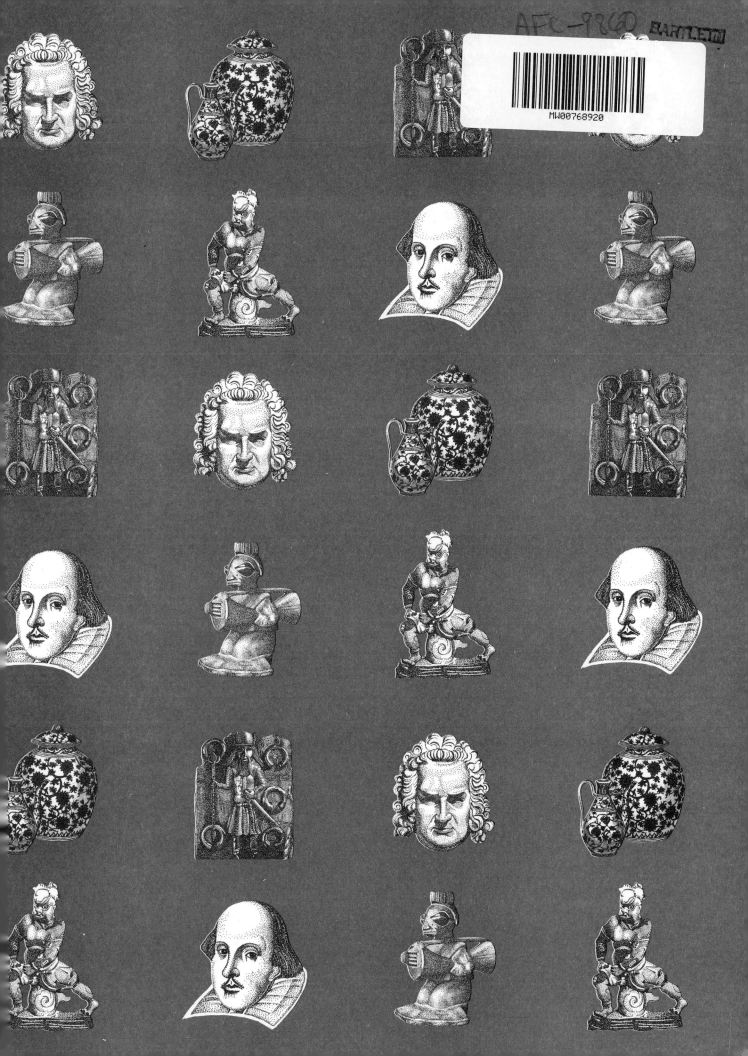

THE
AGE OF DISCOVERY

Brian and Brenda Williams

Illustrated by James Field

PETER BEDRICK BOOKS

NEW YORK

TIMELINK: THE AGE OF DISCOVERY

PETER BEDRICK BOOKS
2112 Broadway
New York, New York 10023

Library of Congress Cataloging-in-Publication
Data

Williams, Brian, 1943-
    Age of Discovery / Brian and Brenda Williams;
    illustrated by James Field.
    64p. 28 × 21.4 cm -- (Timelink)
    Includes index.
    ISBN 0-87226-311-8
    1. History, Modern -- 16th century -- Juvenile
    literature.   2. History, Modern -- 17th century
    -- Juvenile literature   3. History, Modern --
    18th century -- Juvenile literature. [History,
    Modern -- 16th century.   2. History, Modern
    -- 17th century.   3. History, Modern -- 18th
    century.]   I. Williams, Brenda.   II. Field,
    James, 1959-   III. Title.   IV. Series.
    D208.W528   1994
    909.08--dc20   94-18 459
                                        CIP

Printed in China
97 96 95 94 1 2 3 4

Courtiers at the Palace
of Versailles in France in
about 1700 – see pages
40 to 41.

CONTENTS

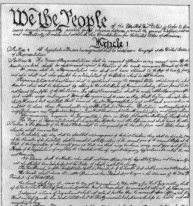

Left: Part of the
American Constitution of
1787 – see pages 56-57.

INTRODUCTION

This book is an introduction to the greatest events in world history from the time when Europeans began to settle in the New World of the Americas until the period of revolutions in America and France which reshaped the world. It is arranged in seven chapters and follows the time sequence from AD 1500 to 1789. Each chapter includes an overview of world events, short features on, for instance, important empires and battles, and extended features on a variety of subjects of special interest. These include the Renaissance, Muslim empires and the Industrial Revolution.

Age of Discovery is the third title in the Timelink series, which is designed to give young readers an overall view of different peoples and their histories, and the links between states and civilizations across the globe. One book cannot describe in detail all that happened everywhere in the world during a period of tremendous change. But this book does show many of the significant turning points – the great events that changed the way people lived then and have influenced the way we live today.

Throughout **Age of Discovery** there are many maps, illustrations, diagrams, photographs and timecharts. The maps show the rise and fall of nation-states, the spread of empires and trade, and voyages of discovery.

Left: Canals, steam-pumps, coal-burning fires and chimney stacks were part of the industrial scene of eighteenth-century western Europe – see pages 48-49.

The illustrations help bring to life dramatic events and show how people lived – their clothes, buildings, arts and sciences, and everyday activities. The timecharts list the dates of important happenings around the world. At the back of the book, two larger timecharts cover the whole of the period of the Age of Discovery for quick, easy reference. A Glossary of unusual words, which are also explained in the text, is included.

Finding out about the past
How do we know what happened before there were sound recordings, films or television to record events? From the 1500s written records (books, legal documents, newspapers and diaries) became more plentiful. These are of great help to us today. Also people were becoming more interested in history, the story of the past. They wrote about the past and about their own times, and their accounts are invaluable to historians of today. Artists drew and painted pictures of important events, such as battles, and portraits of famous people – there are some in this book.

From this evidence, in words and pictures, you can judge for yourself the effect on the world of the great events during the Age of Discovery.

DATES AND PERIODS

All the dates in this book are based on a calendar which has the birth of Jesus Christ as its starting point. Events happening after the birth of Christ are counted forwards from it. They are given the letters AD from the Latin words *anno domini* meaning 'in the year of the Lord'. In this book all the dates are AD.

Revolutions
You will often come across the term 'Revolution' in history books. A revolution is a 'turning around', which in history means a time of great changes, affecting the way countries are governed and the way people live. Three important events described in this book are called Revolutions: the Industrial Revolution, the American Revolution and the French Revolution. Other events during the Age of Discovery could also be called revolutions. Among them are the Reformation (a religious upheaval) in Europe, the overthrow of the Ming emperors in China, the war between Parliament and King in England in the 1640s, and the revolution in ideas about the Universe started by scientists such as Copernicus, Galileo and Newton.

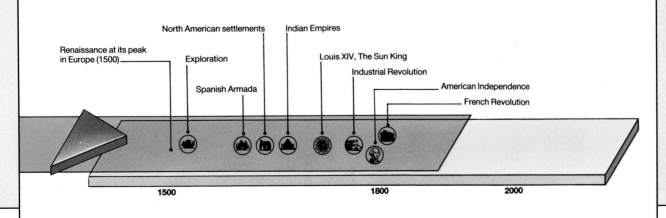

Renaissance at its peak in Europe (1500)
North American settlements
Exploration
Spanish Armada
Indian Empires
Louis XIV, The Sun King
Industrial Revolution
American Independence
French Revolution

1500   1800   2000

THE CHANGING WORLD

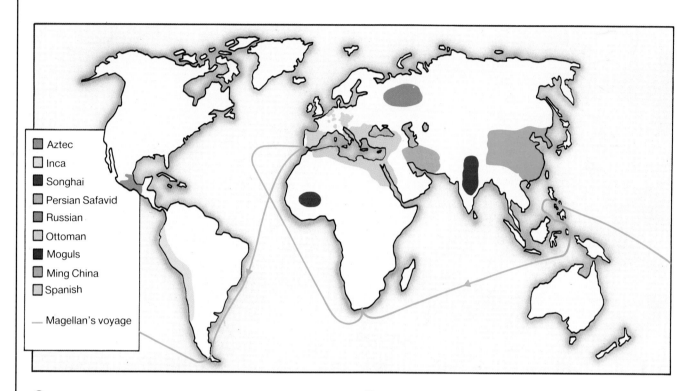

Legend:
- Aztec
- Inca
- Songhai
- Persian Safavid
- Russian
- Ottoman
- Moguls
- Ming China
- Spanish
- — Magellan's voyage

▲ EMPIRES AND NEW WORLDS 1500s

New and Old Worlds – America and Eurasia – met. This was an age of powerful and warlike empires in America, Europe, Africa and Asia. When empires clashed, the stronger one conquered – Spain in Mexico, the Moguls in India. An expedition led by Magellan sailed round the world.

▼ DISCOVERIES AND COLONIES IN THE 1600s

European nations explored and colonized America, and became rivals for overseas trade and territory. Russia expanded eastwards. The Muslim empires of Persia, Turkey and India remained strong. In the Far East, Japan, like its huge neighbour, China, remained isolated.

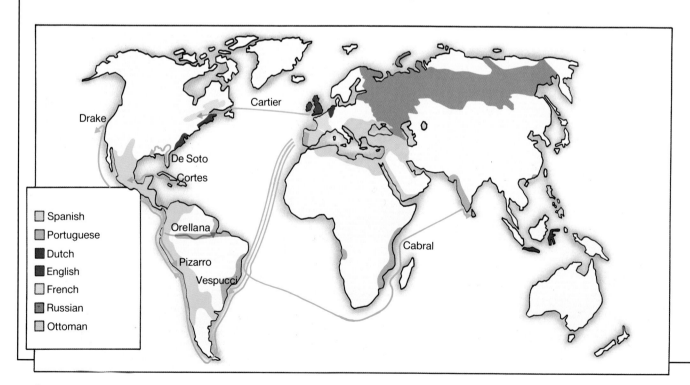

Labels on map: Cartier, Drake, De Soto, Cortes, Orellana, Pizarro, Vespucci, Cabral

Legend:
- Spanish
- Portuguese
- Dutch
- English
- French
- Russian
- Ottoman

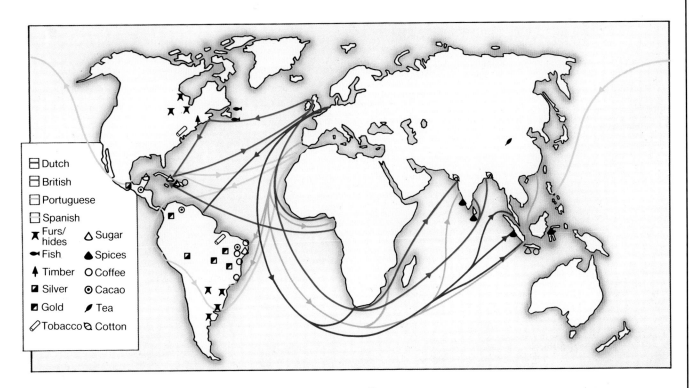

⬆ EUROPEAN WORLD TRADE IN THE 1700s

European ships traded worldwide for raw materials, foods and gold. Britain and France fought for empires in North America and India. The Dutch controlled the East Indies. New nations were growing in North America. South America remained under Spanish and Portuguese control.

⬇ WORLD POWERS AND COLONIES 1760–1789

The first colony was founded in Australia, following several great voyages of Pacific exploration. Britain had by now ousted France from India and Canada. The United States emerged from the American Revolution, while the French Revolution shook the foundations of Europe.

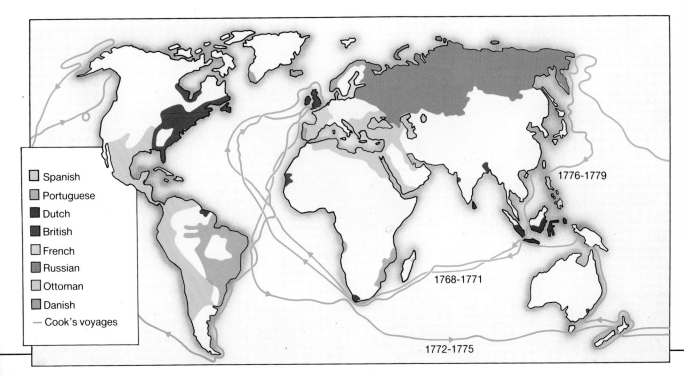

NEW WORLDS

In 1492 Christopher Columbus's voyage from Spain to America opened up the 'New World' to Europeans. It also began a new chapter in exploration: west to America, south around the tip of Africa and east across the Indian Ocean to Asia. Between 1519 and 1522 the survivors of an expedition led by Ferdinand Magellan became the first people to sail around the world (see right).

Spain and Portugal led the way in Europe's voyages of exploration. By the Treaty of Tordesillas (1494), the two countries agreed to divide up between them the lands that they found. Brazil was allotted to Portugal, while the Spanish claimed most of the rest of America. In 1513 a Spanish expedition led by Juan Ponce de Leon, who had sailed with Columbus, landed at the site of what is today Florida in the United States and began to explore the mainland in search of gold.

▼ROUND THE WORLD

The Portuguese Ferdinand Magellan (c.1480–1521) was the first European to sail across the great ocean he named Pacific (meaning 'peaceful'). Because he felt unrewarded for his earlier voyages on behalf of Portugal's rich spice trade, he offered his services to the king of Spain. Under a treaty of 1494, Spain and Portugal divided all newly discovered lands between them – Portugal to the east, and Spain to the west. By sailing west, Magellan hoped to prove that the East Indies spice islands were Spanish, not Portuguese. In 1519 Magellan's ships left harbour – and set a course to sail round the world. Magellan himself was killed in the Philippines, and only one of his five ships returned, three years later, with 19 of the original 227 crew members. The 50,220 mile voyage had proved that the world was round.

Magellan's ship rounding the tip of South America to enter the Pacific

Magellan's voyage

△ Magellan's epic voyage included the first crossing of the Pacific by Europeans. While Europe was convulsed by religious quarrels following Martin Luther's Reformation, European gold-seekers conquered Mexico and Peru. In the East, great Muslim rulers such as Suleiman and Babur governed vast empires.

Luther
Babur
Suleiman
Aztecs
Pizarro
Magellan

Pizarro the conqueror

◐ PIZARRO AND THE INCAS

In Peru an all-powerful god-emperor called the Inca ruled a highly organized, well-governed empire of 6 million people. The land, which was all owned by the state, had excellent roads, providing good communications for trade. The Incas were skilled at crafts and were fine builders, as can be seen from their ruined stone cities. In 1533, 180 Spaniards led by Francisco Pizarro ended Inca rule. The Spanish had the advantages of horses and guns, and the Incas were already weakened by civil war. Pizarro captured the emperor, Atahualpa, ransomed him and then killed him.

▼ FALL OF THE AZTECS

The mighty Aztec Empire flourished in Mexico in the 1400s and early 1500s. This was an advanced civilization, but one ruled by religion. The Aztecs built huge temples where ceremonies were held in which priests made human sacrifices, mostly of slaves and prisoners of war. Spanish treasure-seekers landed in Mexico in 1518, led by Hernando Cortes. The next year, Cortes, with 600 soldiers and local rebels, marched on the Aztec capital, Tenochtitlan (the site of modern Mexico City). Cortes imprisoned the Aztec emperor Montezuma, who mistook him for a god, and by 1521 the Spaniards were the new rulers of Mexico.

Aztec sacrificial ceremony

The treasure-hunters

North America's forests and lakes also attracted other European explorers. In 1535 the Frenchman Jacques Cartier sailed into the St Lawrence River (Canada). He, too, hoped to find gold, but instead found timber, furs and hostile local people. In Central and South America Spanish soldiers did find treasure, and seized it from the people living there and often murdered them.

The Spaniards swiftly and savagely conquered the Aztec and Maya civilizations of Mexico and the Incas of Peru, killing or enslaving the local people (see left). Ships weighed down with gold and silver returned to Spain. There King Charles V, who as Holy Roman Emperor also ruled much of Europe, was waging expensive wars. The gold taken from America was used to help pay for these military campaigns.

1500–1525	1525–1550
1500 Renaissance at its height in Italy. Ismail I founds Safavid dynasty in Persia. **1501** Portuguese begin exploration of Brazil. **1502** Columbus makes fourth and last voyage to America. **1509** First Spanish settlement of American mainland. **1513** The Spaniard Balboa first European to see Pacific Ocean. **1517** Luther issues his 95 theses – start of Reformation in Europe. **1519** Charles V becomes Holy Roman Emperor. **1519** Cortes begins conquest of Aztecs. **1520** Suleiman the Magnificent becomes Ottoman sultan. **1521** Aztec Empire falls to Spaniards. **1522** First round-the-world voyage, by Magellan's crew. **1524** Peasants' War in Germany.	**1526** Moguls defeat Delhi sultan at battle of Panipat. **1526** Ottoman Turks defeat Louis II of Bohemia and Hungary at battle of Mohacs. **1529** Treaty of Cambrai between France and Spain: France gives up its claim to Italy. **1529** Suleiman the Magnificent besieges Vienna, but is driven back. **1530** Humayun succeeds Babur as Mogul emperor. **1534** Henry VIII makes himself head of the Church in England. **1535** Spaniards complete their conquest of Incas. **1535** Cartier explores the St Lawrence River in Canada. **1536** Dissolution of the monasteries in England. **1541** Geneva becomes a Calvinist (Protestant) city. **1545** Council of Trent, start of Counter-Reformation. **1547** Ivan 'the Terrible' crowned Tsar of Russia.

Mighty Asian rulers

Asia, too, was in the turmoil of war and conquest. In 1517 the Ottoman Turks captured Egypt and Syria. Turkish armies terrified Europe when they overran Hungary and almost captured the Austrian city of Vienna. Their leader, Suleiman I, was known as 'the Magnificent' (see page 11).

Meanwhile in Afghanistan a young king named Babur was building another empire. Babur was descended from the famous Mongol conquerors of the 1300s. By 1526 he was ruler of a new Mogul (from the word 'Mongol') empire in India (see page 11).

The Reformation

Europe was emerging from the Middle Ages into a world where people no longer shared the same ideas or beliefs. In 1517 a German monk named Martin Luther publicly protested at the way the Catholic Church was run (see page 11). Luther's supporters were known as Protestants. Their actions started the religious upheaval known as the Reformation. Another form of Protestant ideas, called Calvinism, began in Switzerland.

Meanwhile the English King Henry VIII broke with the Roman Catholic Church because it would not grant him a divorce. To help check the spread of Protestantism, the Church founded a new order of missionary priests, the Jesuits. It also revived the Inquisition court, to root out heresies (ideas that the Church did not accept).

New ideas

Across Europe arts and sciences were being reshaped by the Renaissance (see pages 12–13). It changed the way that people saw themselves and the world. Scientists and philosophers began to question old ideas. The long-held belief that the Earth was the centre of the Universe was challenged by Copernicus, a Polish astronomer.

EUROPE	ASIA	AFRICA	AMERICA
1500 Italian Renaissance at its height. **1508–12** Michelangelo paints Sistine Chapel ceiling. **1517** Luther nails his 95 theses to the door of Wittenberg Church, Germany. **1519** Charles V of Spain Holy Roman Emperor. **1524–25** Peasants' War in Germany. **1526** Battle of Mohacs, Ottomans overrun Hungary. **1529** Turks besiege Vienna. **1534** Henry VIII of England breaks with Rome. Ignatius Loyola founds the Jesuits. **1536–39** Dissolution of monasteries by Henry VIII. **1541** Calvin founds Reformed Church at Geneva, Switzerland. **1543** Copernicus publishes *Revolution of Celestial Bodies*. **1545** Council of Trent: start of Counter-Reformation. **1547** Ivan the Terrible becomes Tsar of Russia.	**1500** Shah Ismail founds Safavid dynasty in Persia. **1509** Battle of Diu gives Portuguese control of Indian Ocean. **1513** Portuguese reach Canton. **1514** War between Turkey and Persia. **1516** Ottomans overrun Syria, Egypt and, in 1517, Arabia. **1526** Battle of Panipat; Babur defeats Delhi sultan and founds Mogul dynasty in India. **1530** Humayun succeeds Babur as Mogul emperor. **1534** Turks capture Mesopotamia. **1539** Guru Nanak, founder of Sikhism, dies. **1540** Humayun exiled to Persia. **1542** Portuguese introduce muskets to Japan. **1549** Francis Xavier is first Christian missionary to Japan. **1550** Mongol Altan-khan invades north China.	**1500** African slaves taken by Europeans for work in New World. **1505** Portuguese establish trading posts in East Africa and Malabar coast, and colonize Mozambique. **1513** Portuguese explore Zambezi river and found trading posts at Sena and Tete. **1517** Ottoman Turks capture Cairo. Mameluke Empire in Egypt ends. **1520** Portuguese mission to Ethiopia. **1534** Turks seize Tunis in North Africa. **1535** Charles V, Holy Roman Emperor, captures Tunis for Europe. **1546** Destruction of Mali Empire by Songhai.	**1501** Slaves from Africa taken to Spanish settlements in New World. **1503** Spanish conquer Puerto Rico. **1507** Martin Waldseemuller's world map is the first to show South America separate from Asia. **1511–15** Spanish conquer Cuba. **1519** Cortes begins conquest of Aztecs. **1520** Chocolate brought from Mexico to Spain. **1521** Aztecs defeated by Spanish. **1521** Spanish begin colonization of Venezuela. **1525** Civil war in Peru. Inca Empire is divided. **c.1525** Potatoes first brought to Europe. **1532** Portuguese start to settle Brazil. **1533** Spanish kill Inca king Atahualpa and capture Inca city of Cuzco. **1535** Spain completes conquest of Inca Empire. **1545** Silver mines found in Peru and Mexico.

Suleiman besieging Budapest, Hungary

Babur in his garden

⊛ SULEIMAN THE MAGNIFICENT

Suleiman I (1494–1566), ruler of the Ottoman Empire from 1520, was called 'Law-giver' by his own people, and 'Magnificent' in western Europe because of his splendid court and brilliant military victories. In Asia his armies invaded Persia (Iran) and captured Baghdad (in Iraq). In Europe he took the island of Rhodes in 1522, crossed the Danube into Hungary and won the battle of Mohacs in 1526. His siege of Vienna in 1529 threatened western Europe, while his fleets controlled the Mediterranean, Red Sea and Persian Gulf. At its height, his empire covered 1 million sq miles.

⊛ BABUR, FIRST MOGUL EMPEROR

Babur ruled most of northern India from 1526 until his death in 1530. Born in what is now Afghanistan, he warred with rival chieftains, not always successfully, before capturing Samarkand, the capital of his great ancestor Tamerlane. From there he moved south into India, using artillery to deadly effect against those who opposed him. In 1526 his invasion force of 12,000 men crushed the far more numerous army of the sultan of Delhi at Panipat. With this victory, Babur gained a new empire in India, which he ruled wisely and well till his death four years later.

DISCOVERY

1500 Pedro Alvares Cabral sails to Brazil, claiming it for Portugal.
1501–2 Amerigo Vespucci explores coast of Brazil.
1502 Columbus discovers Nicaragua.
1513 Vasco Nuñez de Balboa is first European to see Pacific Ocean, after crossing Isthmus of Panama.
1513 Ponce de Leon explores Florida.
1519 Magellan begins voyage around the world.
1522 Survivors of Magellan's voyage return home to Spain.
1522–33 Spanish explore Pacific coast of South America.
1535 Jacques Cartier of France navigates the St Lawrence River, Canada.
1535 Spanish explorers in Chile.
1541 Hernando de Soto discovers the Mississippi river.
1541 Francisco de Orellana explores Amazon river.

▶ LUTHER AND HIS THESES

A priest selling indulgences

Martin Luther (1483–1546) was the son of a copper miner. He attended university before becoming a monk. Luther believed that faith in God mattered more than a person's good deeds. He thought that the Church had become corrupt, especially through the practice of selling indulgences (accepting 'payments for sins'). Luther protested by listing 95 arguments against the practice. He was later excommunicated (expelled from the Church). So began the Protestant movement. He also translated the Bible into German.

THE RENAISSANCE

The word 'renaissance' means rebirth. The European Renaissance marks the end of the Middle Ages and the beginning of modern history. Explorers, politicians, poets, painters, architects and astronomers were all inspired by the Renaissance spirit.

Universities flourished in Europe at this time. Students studied texts from the libraries of the old Roman Empire. Many books were brought from Constantinople to the West by scholars fleeing the city after it fell to the Turks in 1453. Printing with movable type was invented in Germany in 1454 by Johannes Gutenberg. It made books cheaper to produce and allowed ideas to be spread more widely.

The arts

In medieval painting, human figures had appeared flat and not especially lifelike. Renaissance painters and sculptors showed people as they really looked. The early 1500s were the height of the Italian Renaissance, when three artistic geniuses – Raphael, Michelangelo and Leonardo da Vinci – were all at work. Northern painters, such as Dürer, a German, came to Italy to study and learn. Architects copied and improved on ancient Greek and Roman buildings.

△ Italy was the birthplace of the Renaissance. Venice had long been a meeting place of East and West. Florence, Venice, Genoa, and other European cities became famous centres of art and learning and power.

▷ Michelangelo painting the ceiling of the Sistine Chapel. Working alone most of the time, standing or lying on scaffolding, he spent four years on the huge task of covering the ceiling with scenes from the Bible.

Questioning spirits

The Dutch scholar Erasmus tried to find common ground between ancient Greek 'pagan' ideas and the teachings of the Christian Church. Machiavelli, an Italian politician and author, presented new ideas on how to govern a state. Engineers sketched new machines. Some of them, such as Leonardo's 'helicopter', were far ahead of their time. The Renaissance scientists were often also successful artists. Leonardo was equally gifted as painter, scientist and engineer.

THE REBIRTH OF LEARNING

1500 Leonardo da Vinci becomes chief engineer and architect to the ruler of Florence, Cesare Borgia.
1503 Leonardo paints the famous portrait, the *Mona Lisa*.
1505 Germany's most gifted artist, Albrecht Dürer, studies painting in Venice, now the centre of the Italian Renaissance: its artists include Bellini, Titian and Giorgione. Venetian glass, made to a secret formula, is sold all over Europe.
1506 Work begins on St Peter's Basilica in Rome.
1508 Raphael and Michelangelo at height of their powers: Raphael paints *School of Athens* 1511; Michelangelo paints the ceiling of the Sistine Chapel in Rome.
1516 Thomas More's book *Utopia* describes an ideal world.
1516 Erasmus, Dutch humanist and critic of the Church, edits the New Testament of the Bible from the original Greek text.
1526 William Tyndale publishes the first Bible in English (translated from Greek).
1528 Baldassar Castiglione's *The Book of the Courtier* describes the ideal 'Renaissance man'.
1532 Ariosto, an Italian poet, publishes romantic poem, *Orlando Furioso*, celebrating the medieval legendary hero Roland.
1532 Machiavelli's book on statecraft, *The Prince*, is published, five years after Machiavelli's death.

◁ Desiderius Erasmus (c. 1466–1536) was Europe's most famous Renaissance scholar. This Dutchman also did much to inspire the Reformation, though he never became a Protestant himself. Erasmus spoke and wrote in Latin.

DANIEL

△ Hans Holbein the Younger, who was German, painted this picture, *The Ambassadors*, in 1533. The two men here seem to represent all that the Renaissance stood for: confidence, knowledge, inquiry, power. The objects shown – scientific and artistic – emphasize their all-round interests.

NEW NATIONS

In 1556 prince Akbar, then only 13 years old, became emperor of Mogul India. He inherited only a small portion of the lands once ruled by his grandfather Babur (see pages 10, 11), but through conquest and wise rule Akbar created such a powerful empire that he was known, even in faraway Europe, as the 'Great Mogul'.

In 1556, at Panipat, Akbar defeated a Hindu army, and by 1577 he had established the Mogul Empire in northern India. In peacetime he encouraged different religions and art and literature, which flourished under his rule. He himself even introduced a new style of architecture. Akbar is considered to have been the greatest of all the Mogul emperors (see below).

Japan's strong ruler

Elsewhere in Asia another soldier was uniting his people by conquest. Toyotomi Hideyoshi ruled Japan from 1585, putting an end to the civil wars that for 200 years had raged in the country. Hideyoshi was born a peasant, but rose through the army, from foot soldier to samurai warrior (see page 15). He served a *daimyo*, or lord, who recognized him as a courageous soldier. On his lord's death, Hideyoshi took his place and set about conquering the whole of Japan.

By 1590 he had united the nation. He reduced the number of its forts and forbade anyone except the nobility to carry weapons. He created an orderly society that changed little in 350 years.

An elephant race in Mogul India

⦿ THE INDIA OF AKBAR

Akbar the Great (1542–1605) succeeded his father Humayun as Mogul emperor in 1556. He was the most admired and powerful of all India's Mogul rulers. He enlarged the empire by shrewd diplomacy and war, conquering new territories such as Gujarat and Bengal and sending his armies into southern India. He reorganized the government and improved the systems for collecting taxes. Akbar was a Muslim, but tolerant of people of other religions, especially India's Hindus. The trickle of Europeans arriving in India increased during Akbar's reign, and he even invited Portuguese Christian missionaries to come to his court and discuss their religion with him.

△ The Mogul Empire reached a high point under Emperor Akbar. In Japan, Hideyoshi brought peace and stability. Europe was torn by religious and civil strife and wars between Protestants and Catholics.

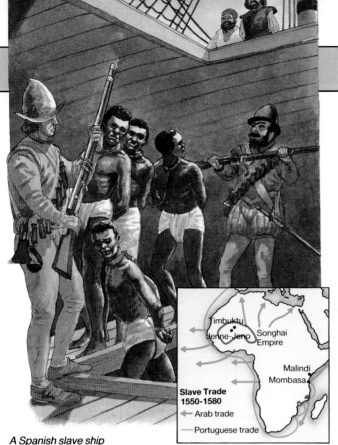

A Spanish slave ship

Africa and the slave trade

Muslim and Christian traders shared an interest in Africa as well as in India. Since the 7th century, Arabs had explored the African coast, gradually moving inland. Camel caravans trekked across the Sahara Desert carrying cloth and salt. African kingdoms such as Songhai (see below left) grew rich from control of the desert trade-routes.

Towns like Timbuktu were prosperous and well-defended. But many people living in villages fell victim to raids by slave-traders (also called slavers). Some slavers were Africans; others were Arabs and Europeans. The Arabs sold slaves to the Ottoman Empire, which controlled much of North Africa, including Egypt. Europeans transported

⏶ BLACK EMPIRES AND SLAVES

By the 1500s Songhai was the most important empire in West Africa. Under Askia Muhammad (ruled 1492–1528) it grew rich from trade. Muslim merchants crowded into the cities of Timbuktu and Jenne-Jeno, which were also centres of learning. Songhai's power collapsed in 1591, when its army was defeated by Moroccans, supported by the Portuguese and Spanish. Many black Africans became victims of the slave trade run by Europeans and Arabs. Captives were taken in chains north across the Sahara, or west to the sea, where ships waited to carry them to the plantations and mines of America.

⏷ SAMURAI JAPAN

In 1543 Portuguese sailors were the first Europeans to visit Japan, the mysterious 'Zipangu' that Marco Polo had heard of during his stay in China nearly 300 years earlier. A Spanish priest, Francis Xavier, arrived in Japan in 1549, to preach Christianity. The Japanese at first welcomed the westerners, who found a country divided by rival lords called *daimyos*, and their warriors, the samurai. Samurai warriors were bound by a strict code of honour – they would rather kill themselves than surrender – and were fiercely loyal to their lord. They wore armour and fought with long swords, refusing to use muskets.

Samurai at war

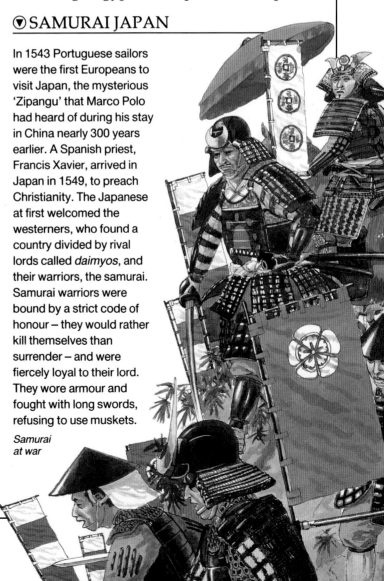

1550–1575

1552–1556 France and Spain at war.
1556 Charles V abdicates. Philip II becomes King of Spain and Netherlands. Charles's brother Ferdinand is made Holy Roman Emperor.
1558 Elizabeth I becomes Queen of England.
1563 Council of Trent ends with no agreement between Catholics and Protestants.
1568 Revolt in the Netherlands against Spain.
1571 Battle of Lepanto: Europeans defeat Turks.
1572 Massacre of Protestants in France.

1575–1600

1580 Francis Drake completes round-the-world voyage.
1582 Pope Gregory XIII's reformed calendar.
1582 Hideyoshi succeeds Oda Nobunaga in Japan.
1585 War of Three Henrys in France: Henry III, Henry of Navarre, Henry of Guise.
1587 Elizabeth I executes Mary, Queen of Scots.
1588 Defeat of Spanish Armada.
1589 Henry of Navarre becomes King of France.
1598 Edict of Nantes, granting French Protestants freedom of worship.

Ivan greeting Richard Chancellor

slaves across the sea to the New World, where they were sold as labourers. Those captives who survived the voyage had little hope of seeing their homeland again.

England's defiant queen

English sea captains were keen to take their share of any ocean trade, including slaves. Henry VIII was not greatly interested in new worlds, but his daughter Elizabeth I (see below), who succeeded Mary I, saw a chance to challenge Spain and enrich her treasury.

Spain ruled the American sea routes, called the Spanish Main, and its warships patrolled the high seas. To avoid them, English seamen looked for a new route to Asia. Some sailed northeast but could not penetrate the Arctic ice. One trader, Richard Chancellor, reached Russia and met the tsar, Ivan 'the Terrible', who was keen to begin trading with the West (see right).

▲ IVAN 'THE TERRIBLE'

Ivan IV (1530–1584) was the first ruler to call himself 'tsar' (emperor) of all Russia. His father had been merely the Grand Duke of Muscovy. Ivan at first ruled well. Eager to modernize his backward country, he welcomed the English traveller Richard Chancellor, and in 1555 the Muscovy Company was set up to sell English cloth in exchange for Russian timber and tar. Later Ivan became cruel and violent. He saw enemies on all sides, especially among Russia's landowners or boyars. In his rages Ivan ordered dreadful massacres and even killed his own son.

▶ ELIZABETH OF ENGLAND

Elizabeth I of England

Henry VIII's youngest daughter, Elizabeth (1533–1603), came to the throne in 1558. Her reign was an English 'golden age'. England defeated the Spanish Armada, English sailors roved the oceans, and in London people flocked to see the plays of Shakespeare. Elizabeth stayed unmarried, but kept Europe in suspense about her choice of husband. Fearing plots against her, Elizabeth reluctantly ordered the execution of her Catholic cousin Mary Queen of Scots in 1587. However, Mary's son, James, became England's next monarch.

EUROPE

1553 Mary I becomes Queen of England, marries Philip of Spain in 1554.
1556 Habsburg lands divided between Philip of Spain and Charles V's brother Ferdinand.
1558 France regains Calais, last English territory in France.
1567 Duke of Alva becomes Spain's governor of the Netherlands.
1568 Start of Netherlands revolt against Spain.
1572 St Bartholomew's Day massacre in France. Many Protestants are killed.
1576 Antwerp sacked by Spanish troops.
1580 Spain annexes Portugal.
1581 Foundation of Dutch Republic, with William the Silent as its ruler.
1585 War of Three Henrys in France.
1588 Defeat by English of the Spanish Armada.
1594 Tyrone leads Irish rebellion against English rule.

Attack on a Protestant house

◉ PROTESTANT MASSACRE

In the 1500s France was torn by religious and political rivalries. In August 1572 many Huguenots (French Protestants) gathered in Paris to celebrate the wedding of their leader, Henry of Navarre. The Catholic leader Henry of Guise, in league with the king's mother, Catherine de Medici, persuaded King Charles IX that the Protestants were about to revolt. Early on 24 August, St Bartholomew's Day, many Huguenot leaders were murdered though Henry of Navarre was spared. Mobs took to the streets and within hours thousands of Protestants lay dead.

Protestants and Catholics

The Reformation had split Europe into two opposing and often warring camps, each intolerant of the other's religion. Both sides behaved cruelly. People were tortured to make them change their beliefs, and those who were brave enough to resist were often killed in the most horrible ways. In England, when Queen Mary I, a Catholic, was on the throne, the Protestants suffered. Under Elizabeth I, who was a Protestant, the Catholics were persecuted.

France, weakened after years of war against the Holy Roman Empire, now became a victim of civil wars. Although France was a Catholic kingdom, many of the French supported the Reformation and became Protestants. They were called Huguenots and were persecuted by the government. Civil war broke out, and there were massacres on both sides (see left).

ASIA

1540s Portuguese are first Europeans to land in Japan.
1552–56 Russians move into Kazan and Astrakhan.
1557 Portuguese set up trading base at Macao, China.
1560s Spain takes control of the Philippines.
1565 Akbar extends Mogul rule into southern India.
1565 Turks besiege Malta.
1566 Death of Suleiman the Magnificent.
1568–1600 Japan unified after civil wars.
1571 Turkish fleet defeated at battle of Lepanto.
1575 Akbar the Great conquers Bengal.
1581 Russian settlement of Siberia begins.
1585 Hideyoshi becomes ruler of Japan.
1587 Shah Abbas I becomes ruler of Persia.
1592 Japan invades Korea but has to withdraw.
1600 English East India Company founded.

AFRICA

1562 English slavers take African slaves from Sierra Leone to Hispaniola.
1571 Bornu Empire in West Africa begins to gain power under Sultan Idris.
1571 Portuguese found colony in Angola, southern Africa.
1573 Don John of Austria regains Tunis from Turks, who recapture it in 1574.
1578 Moroccans defeat Portuguese at battle of Al Kasr al Kebir.
1591 Moroccans with European mercenaries and guns defeat army of Songhai at battle of Tondibi; this defeat ends Songhai kingdom.

AMERICA

1550 Brazil has a Portuguese governor-general (1549) representing the king.
1564 Spanish ships begin carrying silver back from America to Europe.
1567 Portuguese found Rio de Janeiro in Brazil.
1576 Martin Frobisher of England fails to find a North-West Passage to Asia.
1578 Drake sails through Straits of Magellan and explores Pacific coast of America, attacking Spanish ships.
1579 Drake is first European to see west coast of Canada.
1583 Gilbert founds English colony in Newfoundland.
1586 Drake leads English expedition to the West Indies.
1598 Juan de Onate of Spain explores American Southwest.

ARTS, SCIENCE

1561 Birth of Francis Bacon, English statesman and scientist.
1564 Birth of William Shakespeare.
1567 Birth of Italian composer Monteverdi.
1577 Peter Paul Rubens, Flemish painter, born.
1575–80 Spanish writer Cervantes is prisoner of the Turks.
1582 Reformed calendar introduced by Pope Gregory XIII.
1589 William Lee (England) designs a knitting machine.
1590–1613 Shakespeare writing his plays.
1590 Janssen (Netherlands) invents the microscope.
1590 Edmund Spenser, English poet, writes *Faerie Queen*.
1592 Galileo invents thermometer.
1593 Marlowe, English dramatist, killed in brawl.
1596 Birth of French philosopher Descartes.

Spanish troops attack a Dutch town

⚜ THE DUTCH REVOLT

The Netherlands formed part of Spain's empire. By the 1550s many Dutch Protestants, especially in the northern provinces, suffered under the rule of Philip II of Spain, the most strongly Catholic monarch in Europe. In 1568 William 'the Silent', Prince of Orange, led a revolt. Spain sent its best troops and commanders to the Netherlands, but the Dutch flooded low-lying land (known locally as the polders) to halt the Spanish armies. William failed to unite all the provinces behind him but led the seven in the north to independence. He was assassinated in 1584.

When, in 1584, a Protestant prince, Henry of Navarre, became heir to the throne, his Catholic enemies were furious, and there was still more bloodshed. In 1589 King Henry III was assassinated, and Henry of Navarre became king. Henry was a peacemaker. He became a Catholic, won Spain's friendship and in 1598 signed the Edict of Nantes, which allowed Huguenots to worship as they pleased. The French wars of religion were over.

Revolt in the Low Countries

Spain was Europe's richest and strongest nation. In the early 1500s the Low Countries (today the Netherlands and Belgium) came under Spanish control when their ruler Charles V became King of Spain at the age of six. In 1568 the Dutch, who were Protestants, revolted against foreign rule and against Spanish Catholicism (see above). King Philip II of Spain, who came to the throne in 1556, wanted to make his people Catholic.

On land the Dutch rebels were outnumbered by Spain's formidable armies, but at sea they were more successful. In 1581 the Dutch declared the northern provinces of the Low Countries an independent republic, and went on fighting Spain until 1648. In the southern provinces (Belgium), which were mostly Catholic, the revolt petered out.

War on land and sea

Land battles had not changed much in two centuries. Soldiers on foot carried a long pike or a halberd (a combined spear and battle-axe). Cavalry fought with swords and lances. Artillery comprised cannon that were clumsy and inaccurate at a distance. Smaller hand-guns, called muskets, could fire only one shot before being reloaded.

Sea battles, however, were changing. Spain had new and larger warships: three-masted galleons that sailed faster than other nations' cumbersome medieval warships. Cannon were ranged along the galleon's

▶ THE SPANISH ARMADA

In 1588, 130 Spanish ships sailed for England. This was the mighty Armada, which Philip II believed was invincible. Its mission was to collect an army from the Netherlands and invade England. The English assembled 197 ships, smaller but with longer-range cannon. Unfavourable winds plus an English attack with fire-ships scattered the Armada and broke its formation. Trapped off the Low Countries, the surviving Spanish ships fled. Only 76 vessels returned to Spain.

English fire-ships against Spanish galleons

deck to fire broadsides. At the battle of Lepanto, the oared galleys of the Turks were destroyed by cannon fire (see right).

Spain's bid for supremacy

Spain, having built a vast empire in America, defeated its overseas rival Portugal in 1500s. Only the Dutch and the English stood in the way of Spain's domination of Europe. Philip II had married Queen Mary I of England, hoping he could help return England to the Catholic faith. But Mary died in 1558, and her sister Elizabeth, who became Queen, refused to marry anyone. To Philip's annoyance, she supported the Dutch rebels and let her sea captains plunder Spanish gold in Mexico and South America.

Spanish dignity was offended. In 1588 Philip sent a huge fleet to invade England. The Armada, as it was called, set sail proudly, but met with disaster (see above). Its defeat dashed Philip's hopes. He died in 1598, and Spain's golden age moved towards its close.

An armed Spanish galleas

▲ THE BATTLE OF LEPANTO

In 1571 the Turks tried to capture the island of Cyprus from the Venetians. They sailed from their capital, Constantinople, and from harbours they had captured in the Middle East, with a fleet of some 270 galleys. To stop them, Philip II of Spain sent his half-brother Don John of Austria to command a European fleet of 200 ships. It included six galleases (galleys with sails as well as oars) bristling with heavy guns. The fleets fought near Lepanto in Greece on 7 October 1571, and the Turks were defeated. It was the last great sea battle in which galleys were used.

SPAIN'S GOLDEN AGE

In 1512 King Ferdinand seized the kingdom of Navarre, uniting the whole of Spain. Within 30 years Spain had conquered an empire in the New World. This empire reached its height under King Philip II, who ruled from 1556 to 1598.

Spain's overseas empire brought great riches. A single Spanish treasure-ship on one voyage probably carried home more gold than England or its queen could expect to see in a whole year. The Spanish city of Seville, which controlled trade with the colonies, became especially prosperous. But Spain could not by itself produce all the goods that the colonists needed. It had to spend some of its silver and gold to buy from other European countries. It also had to pay out large sums to maintain its huge armies, and its people remained poor.

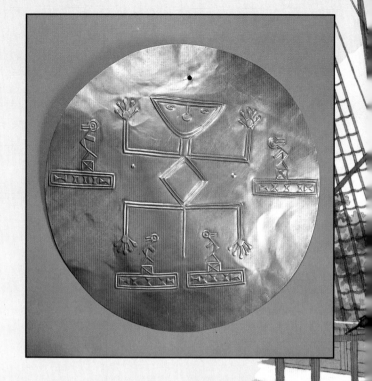

◁ King Philip II of Spain, who promoted exploration and plunder of the Americas.

△ Above: Gold disc taken from Peru by Spanish treasure-hunters. Gold from America helped cause the price rises in Europe that continue to the present day!

Art and literature

Art and religion in Spain were often linked. The Church, particularly the Jesuits, dominated Spanish life. Philip II admired the writings of mystics such as Saint John of the Cross and Saint Teresa of Avila.

Spain's most famous writer is Cervantes (1547–1616), author of *Don Quixote*. He fought the Turks at Lepanto, was captured by pirates, and eventually came home to a job as a grain collector. The greatest painter of Spain's golden age was El Greco ('the Greek'), who originally came from Crete.

△ Spanish possessions in Europe at the time of Philip II, when Spain was Europe's greatest imperial power. Spain and Portugal controlled the New World of the Americas. In 1494 the Pope had divided America, by the Treaty of Tordesillas. This treaty kept Spain out of a large area of eastern South America, but much of the rest, including Peru and Mexico, was under Spanish control by the 1550s.

THE RISE OF SPAIN

1545 Spanish discover silver in America.
1556 Philip II becomes King of Spain.
1559 Peace of Cateau-Cambresis with France.
1562 Lope de Vega, Spanish dramatist, born.
1565 Spain colonizes Philippines.
1568 Netherlands revolt.
1571 Battle of Lepanto.
1576 Greek painter El Greco comes to work in Spain.
1582 Death of St Teresa of Avila.
1582 Escorial Palace, near Madrid, finished, after 20 years.
1591 Aragon submits to Spanish throne. Death of St John of the Cross.
1598 Philip II dies, succeeded by Philip III.

◁ A Spanish ship loading American gold and silver. From 1564 the slow treasure-ships sailed in convoy, with an escort of warships to fight off pirates and English raiders. Ports in the Old World such as Cartagena and Cadiz were fortified against attack.

21

THE QUEST FOR POWER

Europe entered the 17th century amid turmoil and violence. Over much of the continent people suffered the horrors of the Thirty Years' War (1618–1648). This began as a religious conflict between Catholic and Protestant princes but became a confused power struggle between nations. The Holy Roman Empire made a last bid for real power, and failed. Protestant fought Protestant, and Catholic France joined Protestant Sweden against Catholic Spain.

Royal power

The Thirty Years' War was the last great European war to be fought over religion. At its end Spain and Austria were left weaker. France, with nearly 20 million people, was Europe's strongest nation. French policy was guided by the cardinals Richelieu and Mazarin. These two skilful statesmen served kings who believed in absolute power and who sought to increase their power at the expense of the nobles. The nobles protested and then rose up, first in Paris and later in other parts of France. But this protest movement, called the Fronde, failed to check the rise in royal power (see page 23).

New hope in a New World

The quarrel between Protestants and Catholics made life difficult for minority groups. In mainly Protestant England, Catholics received unfair treatment. In France, which was largely Catholic, it was the Protestant Huguenots who suffered.

A group of English Protestants called Puritans believed that true laws came direct from God through the Bible. They wanted a Church that did not depend on wealth and power. Some Puritans turned their back on Europe and sailed to America to begin a new life. In 1620 the little ship *Mayflower* landed a small band of Puritans in Massachusetts, on the east coast of North America (see page 23). There the Pilgrim Fathers, as they came to be known, met friendly Indians who taught them how to survive the harsh winters and plant crops.

They called the region where they settled New England, and it is still known by that name today. In America, Puritans were free to worship as they pleased. Although in law European royal power reached across the ocean to America, the new Americans were mostly left to govern themselves.

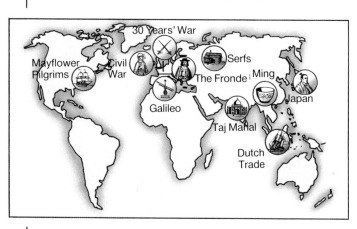

△ Settlers from Europe sailed to North America to escape wars and religious persecution. It was a time of new ideas in science. In China, the Ming Empire ended in 1644. Japan withdrew into isolation, barring foreigners and Christian missionaries.

1600–1625

1600 British found the first European East India Company.
1603 Japan's ruler Hideyoshi dies.
1603 James VI of Scotland becomes James I of England, uniting the countries under one crown.
1605 Jahangir, Akbar's son, is Mogul emperor of India.
1605 German astronomer Kepler publishes his laws of planetary motion.
1607 English found colony in Virginia, America.
1618 Thirty Years' War begins.
1620 *Mayflower* pilgrims land in America.
1624 Richelieu becomes chief minister of France.
1625 Charles I becomes King of England.

1625–1650

1627 Shah Jahan ruler of Mogul India.
1632 Gustavus Adolphus of Sweden killed in battle.
1638 Turks conquer Baghdad.
1639 Japan restricts foreign trade to Dutch and Chinese.
1642 English Civil War begins.
1642 Death of the great scientist Galileo.
1642 Abel Tasman of Holland is first European to sight New Zealand.
1644 Last Ming emperor of China kills himself; Manchus take over.
1645 Venice and Turkey go to war over Crete.
1648 Start of Fronde rebellion in France.
1649 Execution of Charles I of England.

Major English Colonies

Massachusetts 1629
Connecticut 1636
Maryland 1632
New Amsterdam
Virginia 1607

▶ THE PILGRIMS

The *Mayflower* pilgrims founded the second permanent English settlement in America in 1620. The first was in 1607. They came to follow a life of simple Puritan worship and hard work. There were 102 men, women and children on board the *Mayflower*. After 65 days at sea, the Pilgrims landed in New England. They set to work building wooden houses and planting crops. About half the settlers died during the first winter.

Puritans in the New World

Gustavus Adolphus of Sweden

The boy-king Louis fleeing Paris

⦿ THE THIRTY YEARS' WAR

In 1617 a Bohemian Catholic, Ferdinand II, was elected Holy Roman Emperor. The Protestants of Bohemia (today in the Czech Republic) revolted, leading to the Thirty Years' War. Ferdinand's generals, Tilly and Wallenstein, were at first victorious, as Protestant and Catholic nations joined the fighting on one or other side. The Protestants' best general was Sweden's king, Gustavus Adolphus, a master of manoeuvre and artillery. He was killed in 1632. After a short-lived peace in 1635, the war became a struggle between France and Austria and dragged on until 1648. Germany was left in ruins by the experience.

⦿ THE FRONDE

Louis XIV became king of France when still a child. His mother, Anne of Austria, and her Italian chief minister, Cardinal Mazarin, ruled on his behalf. Growing royal power alarmed the nobles and regional parliaments, who feared that their own privileges were being taken away. By 1649 complaints had turned into civil war, known as the Fronde. Louis had to flee from Paris. The Fronde later turned into a squabble between nobles. The king's soldier-cousin, Condé, tried to seize power, but the young king and Mazarin were back in control by 1653. Louis's power as an absolute monarch was never challenged again.

Russian serfs

Poverty and riches in the East

In the east the rulers shared power with no one. The tsar, or emperor, of Russia was an autocrat, meaning that he ruled alone and had total power over his subjects. Nine out of ten Russians were serfs, who were bound by law to work on land that they could never own. Many serfs were treated harshly and lived in extreme poverty (see right).

India under the Moguls was much more splendid than Russia, though there too most people were poor. To European merchants, India promised exotic goods and wealth. On the last day of 1600, the British East India Company was formed, and three years later its official presented himself at the court of the Great Mogul at Agra. When, in 1605, Emperor Akbar died, the Mogul Empire was among the very greatest that the world has ever known.

SERFDOM IN RUSSIA

Compared to western Europe, life in Russia was medieval. The tsars rewarded loyal nobles by giving them land. With the land came the people who farmed it – the serfs. A serf was a slave to the land, and from 1649 some 12 million Russians were bound by the law of serfdom. Many lived in remote villages, in log houses warmed in the long bitter winter by a wood-fuelled stove kept burning day and night. Serfs were uneducated. The land did not provide enough food, and many serfs lived in poverty, comforted only by the Orthodox Church and by ancient superstitions.

EUROPE	ASIA	AFRICA, PACIFIC	AMERICA
1603 Elizabeth I of England dies. James VI of Scotland is crowned James I of England. **1605** Gunpowder plot (to kill James) fails. **1611** Authorized (King James') Version of the Bible published in England. **1613** Romanov dynasty in Russia founded. **1618** Start of Thirty Years' War. **1624–42** Richelieu chief minister of France. **1632** Gustavus Adolphus, soldier-king of Sweden, killed in battle. **1640** Portuguese revolt against Spain. **1641** Catholic uprising in Ireland. **1642** Start of English Civil War. **1643** Louis XIV becomes King of France, Mazarin is chief minister. **1645** Battle of Naseby in English Civil War, end of Charles I's hopes. **1648** Treaty of Westphalia ends Thirty Years' War. **1648** Fronde uprising in France. **1649** Charles I executed. **1649** New laws enforce serfdom in Russia.	**1600** Foundation of English East India Company, followed in 1602 by the Dutch East India Company, and in 1604 by the French. **1603** Death of Hideyoshi, ruler of Japan, who is succeeded by Tokugawa Ieyasu. **1619** Dutch found Batavia (now Jakarta), Indonesia; in 1623 they drive the British from the East Indies. **1628** Start of reign of Mogul emperor Shah Jahan, who builds the Taj Mahal. **1629** Shah Sofi of Persia, start of Persia's decline. **1630s** Japanese kill Christians, ban foreign travel and restrict ties with outside world. **1638** Russian expansion to the Pacific coast. **1638** Turks capture Baghdad. **1641** Dutch capture trade base of Malacca in East Indies from Portuguese. **1644** China's Ming dynasty falls under attack from Manchu invaders; the new Qing dynasty is founded.	**1606** Willem Jansz, a Dutch navigator, and De Torres of Spain separately sight Australia – the first Europeans to do so. **1616** Willem Schouten of Holland sails round Cape Horn into the Pacific. **1619** First black slaves from West Africa taken to Virginia in America. **1621** Dutch capture trading base of Goree in West Africa from Portuguese. **1628** Portuguese destroy Mwenemutapa (Mashona) Empire in central Africa (Zimbabwe). **1637** Dutch take Elmina in West Africa from Portuguese. **1642** Abel Tasman of Holland sees Van Diemen's Land (Tasmania) and New Zealand. **1645** Capuchin monks explore River Congo (now Zaire) in Africa.	**1607** English found settlement of Jamestown in Virginia. **1608** Samuel de Champlain of France explores St Lawrence River and founds Quebec in Canada. **1609** Henry Hudson explores the American river later called the Hudson. **1612** English colonize Bermuda. **1619** Virginians import first black slaves from Africa. **1620** Pilgrim Fathers land in America from the *Mayflower*. **1621** Dutch West Indies Company is founded. **1625** Dutch settle New Amsterdam, later New York. **1634** Jean Nicolet of France explores Lake Michigan and is told by Indians of the mighty Mississippi river. **1641** French explorers and traders move into Michigan area. **1642** French found settlement at Montreal in Canada.

European influence in Asia and the Pacific was spreading. Russian explorers and colonists moved overland eastwards into Siberia, reaching the Pacific coast by 1638. Dutch ships sailed beyond India to the East Indies, where, in 1619, Dutch traders set up a base at Batavia (today called Jakarta) on the island of Java. In 1642 a Dutch sailor, Abel Tasman, discovered Van Diemen's Land (now Tasmania).

China and the West
A few missionaries from Europe tried to convert first the Japanese and then the Chinese to Christianity. Matteo Ricci, an Italian Jesuit priest, and a keen scientist, impressed the Chinese emperor with a gift of a chiming clock and by his skill in astronomy. But the Westerners won few converts. The Chinese were mainly interested in

borrowing scientific skills – such as the secrets of casting stronger cannon.

In 1644 the centuries-old Ming dynasty (see below), was toppled, but life for the Chinese people under their new Manchu rulers continued much as before.

England's king loses his crown
In Europe, change was sometimes dramatic. From 1603 England and Scotland shared the same monarch. James VI of Scotland became James I of England after the death of the childless Queen Elizabeth I. James I's son, Charles I, came to the throne in 1625. A shy, mild-mannered man, he firmly believed in the God-given right of kings to rule. In England, unlike in France, there was a Parliament strong enough and determined enough to oppose a king. But Charles tried first to challenge Parliament and then to rule

ARTS, SCIENCES

c.1603 *Kabuki* theatre begins in Japan.
1605 Cervantes, Spanish writer, publishes first part of *Don Quixote*.
1607 First opera, by the Italian composer Monteverdi.
1609 Kepler describes how the planets move in orbit around the Sun. Galileo makes his own telescope and studies the Moon and planets.
1614 Logarithms invented by John Napier of Scotland.
1620s–1630s Dutch painters Rubens and Rembrandt at height of powers.
1628 William Harvey, an English physician, publishes work on the circulation of the blood.
1630s Velasquez, Spanish painter, works at royal court.
1636 Harvard, the first university in North America, founded.
1642 Pascal, French mathematician, designs an adding machine.
1643 Torricelli of Italy invents the barometer.

⊙ MING CHINA

The Ming dynasty ruled China for nearly 300 years. European visitors marvelled at Chinese technology and art, such as their porcelain (fine pottery). When the northern Manchus invaded China in 1644, the last Ming emperor killed himself. But the invasion had little effect on Chinese civilization.

Ming porcelain

⊙ CIVIL WAR IN ENGLAND

The civil war in England was a struggle for power between Parliament and King. The soldiers of Parliament were known as Roundheads, and many were Puritans. The King's supporters were called Royalists or Cavaliers. Fighting began in 1642. Parliament controlled London and most large towns, and it organized a well-trained professional army. Defeated on the battlefield, King Charles I was tried for high treason and in 1649 he was executed. England became a republic, called the Commonwealth. From 1653 to 1658 the country was ruled by Oliver Cromwell, as Lord Protector. In 1660 the monarchy was restored under Charles II.

Roundhead soldiers

Control of England 1642-1645
mainly Parliament
Royalists
Parliament

25

without it. He was no tyrant, but his foolishness led England into civil war and cost him his throne and his head (see page 25).

The new science

In Europe a scientific revolution was led by the Italian Galileo and the German Johannes Kepler. They believed in experiment, like René Descartes of France, who wrote that a scientist should accept only what he saw and could prove to be true.

Galileo and two of his later telescopes

⊙ GALILEO AND THE TELESCOPE

People had used glass lenses in eyeglasses (spectacles) since the 1300s. Combining two lenses – one convex, the other concave – produces a telescope. This was first done in 1608, probably by accident. The new 'instruments for seeing at a distance' excited scientists across Europe. Until then astronomers had relied on eyesight and mathematics alone. In 1609 Galileo, Italy's leading scientist, made his own telescope. He turned it skywards, and saw to his astonishment what no astronomer had seen before: hundreds of stars too faint to be visible to the naked eye, craters on the Moon, and four moons orbiting the planet Jupiter. Modern astronomy had begun.

▼ THE DUTCH IN THE EAST INDIES

Freed from Spanish rule, in the early 1600s the Dutch vigorously embarked on overseas empire-building. They were expert sailors, and Dutch ships roved the Indian Ocean and the Pacific. The Dutch hoped to drive the Portuguese from the East Indies (modern Indonesia) and fight off the English, who were keen to grab the East Indies trade for themselves. The Dutch made deals with local rulers and established a powerful trade base and settlement at Batavia (now Jakarta) on the island of Java. In 1623 they executed 10 English captives at Amboina to show that they meant business. They took Portugal's main base, Malacca, in 1641.

A Dutch trading ship

▶ JAPANESE THEATRE

Japan was at peace under the Tokugawa shoguns. They built their new capital on the site of a village called Edo. This later became Tokyo. Ever watchful for signs of revolt, the all-powerful shogun made sure that nobles attended the court. When they went home, their families had to remain. But there were palace entertainments to amuse them, such as *kabuki* theatre. This first appeared in the 1600s and is still popular today. *Kabuki* actors, who are all men, wear colourful costumes and act with exaggerated gestures.

A Dutchman named Hans Lippershey is said to have invented the telescope in 1608. Within two years, telescopes were being sold in Germany, Italy and England. The Chinese emperor was given one in 1634. By then Galileo had used a telescope to observe the Moon and the planets (see page 26).

Galileo announced that Copernicus (see page 10) had been right in saying that the Earth orbited the Sun. The Catholic Church in Rome disagreed and imprisoned Galileo for denying the Bible's teachings. Old and sick, he 'confessed' he was wrong, but nothing could stop the spread of the truth.

Japan withdraws, India builds

From 1609 Japan had a new ruler, Tokugawa Ieyasu, a *shogun* (general) who ruled in the name of the emperor but was his own master. The Tokugawa family went on to rule Japan for more than 250 years. All Japan's nobles had to swear loyalty to the shogun.

The Japanese closed their ports to European traders and Christian missionaries. They banned all foreigners, allowing just one Dutch ship a year to visit the port of Nagasaki. But Japanese theatre flourished in the 1600s (see below left).

In India, the Mogul court continued to be open to artists, scientists and thinkers from all over the Islamic world – and beyond. Its most famous monument is the beautiful Taj Mahal (see below).

The Taj Mahal

Japanese kabuki actors

⊙ THE TAJ MAHAL

In 1629 Shah Jahan, India's Mogul emperor, mourned the death of his favourite wife, Mumtaz Mahal. He wanted her tomb to be the most beautiful ever built, and summoned architects from all over the Muslim world to design it. No stone was too costly, no decoration too painstaking. The result was the Taj Mahal at Agra, a serene building in white marble, surrounded by pools and gardens. Twenty thousand workers were hired, yet the building took 20 years to complete. Today the Taj Mahal is India's most famous monument. In a vault beneath the massive central dome the tombs of Shah Jahan (who died in 1666) and his beloved Mumtaz Mahal lie side by side.

MUSLIM EMPIRES

Muslim power grew in the 1600s. There were three great Muslim empires: Ottoman, Mogul and Safavid. The Ottoman Turks advanced westward, at times threatening to take over eastern Europe. The Moguls ruled most of India. The Safavids ruled Persia.

The Persian empire
The Ottomans and Moguls were Sunni Muslims. The Safavid rulers, called shahs, were followers of the breakaway sect, Shi'ism. Shi'ites believe that, after the Prophet Muhammad, came a line of divinely selected leaders called imams, the first of whom was Muhammad's cousin Ali. Sunni Muslims do not accept this, and the Ottomans often fought with the Safavids.

Persian art and trade reached new heights in the reign of Abbas I. He built a beautiful new city at Isfahan, with spacious parks and gardens. Isfahan became famous for its markets and fine carpets.

Mogul magnificence
In Mogul India the emperor Akbar (see page 14) employed painters and architects from all over the Muslim world. But at his new city, Fatehpur Sikri, he hired Indian Hindu masons to decorate the sandstone palaces.

To escape the heat, Mogul rulers used to relax in shady gardens with cooling fountains and ponds. They also loved hunting and, like their Mongol forebears, rode horses from earliest boyhood.

Ottoman Turkey
The Ottoman Empire was the largest of the Muslim empires. Its capital was Istanbul (formerly Constantinople), from where the empire was ruled. Boys were trained to be either janissaries (soldiers fanatically loyal to the sultan) or civil servants, of whom the most powerful was the Grand Vizier, or chief minister.

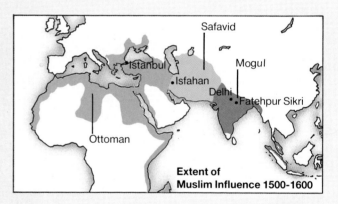

Extent of Muslim Influence 1500-1600

△ The Muslim world stretched from Europe to India, and into Africa.

Foreign visitors marvelled at the magnificent cities built for the Muslim rulers.

◁ The helmet of Shah Abbas I of Persia. Muslim armour and furnishings were finely crafted. Intricate patterns are a feature of Islamic art, like this Turkish fabric (below).

THE RULE OF ISLAM

1602–1618 Holy war between Persia and Turkey.
1603 In Africa, the Bornu Empire (Nigeria) reaches its peak under the sultan Mai Idris Alawma (ruled 1571–1603).
1605 Under Mogul emperor Jahangir, arts flourish in India.
1612 Murad IV becomes sultan of Ottoman Empire at the age of 11; he is a stern warrior who crushes rebels.
1628 Jahangir's third son Shah Jahan succeeds him as Mogul emperor. He builds the Taj Mahal (1630–53) and moves the imperial capital to Delhi in 1648. He also amasses a vast jewel collection.
1629 Death of Shah Abbas brings to an end the greatest period of Safavid Persia's prosperity. Turks and Persians renew border wars over territory.
1638 Ottoman Turks capture Baghdad from Persians: Mesopotamia becomes part of Turkish Empire.
1640 Ottoman Empire left in disarray following the death of Sultan Murad IV. Turkish conquests halted.
1645 Turks begin a long struggle with Venice for control of the island of Crete.

△ Shah Abbas made
Persia great again: his reign
(1588–1629) is famous for
its art, architecture and
religious tolerance. Envoys
and merchants from both
East and West flocked to
his magnificent new capital
of Isfahan.

◁ This painting, from about
1620, shows India's Mogul
emperor Jahangir on a hunt
with his officials and
attendants.

29

FOUNDING THE FUTURE

By the mid-17th century Europe was at a crossroads. After a civil war England had executed its king, Charles I, and become a republic (see page 25). There were wars going on between European powers. The English fought the Spanish and the Dutch, the Swedes opposed the Russians, and the Dutch faced the French in battle. These rivalries also extended to the New World.

Old enmities continued too. The Turks again threatened eastern Europe, as their armies probed the defences of the Holy Roman Empire. In 1683 a Turkish force almost succeeded in capturing the Austrian capital, Vienna (see below right.)

The French and English in America
In the New World, France and Britain were building empires, through colonies and trade. Dutch and Swedes were pushed out. In 1664 England captured the American settlements of New Netherlands and New Sweden (see also page 31).

Spain, too, saw parts of its New World empire gradually disappear. Jamaica was lost to England, and Haiti to France. England's

American colonies stretched along the east coast of what is now the United States. Through the Hudson's Bay Company, founded in 1670, England extended its trade in Canada. Here England and France were rivals. French traders had opened trails and river routes into New France, north of the Great Lakes, and the vast territory of Louisiana in the west (see map).

French power at its peak
In Europe, France was becoming the dominant power. Venice, its past greatness fading, was just a city port. Spain was weakening, and Prussia was as yet no match

⊙ THE SIEGE OF VIENNA

Turkish power, at its peak in the early 1500s under Suleiman the Magnificent (see page 11), had begun to weaken after the naval defeat at the battle of Lepanto (1571). But in eastern Europe, Turkey still held the Balkans (today Greece, Bulgaria, Romania and Serbia) and threatened to swallow Hungary. In 1683 a Turkish army was at the gates of the Austrian capital, Vienna. The city was defended and saved by Poland's soldier-king John Sobieski, ally of the Holy Roman Emperor. Hungary was saved, and the Turkish advance into Europe was halted.

Turkish army besieges Vienna

△ France was Europe's greatest power, fighting costly wars. The French led in exploring North America, where English colonial power was growing on the east coast. The Dutch had a foothold in Southern Africa. China had a new dynasty, and the Mogul Empire was weakening. The Turks still threatened eastern Europe.

for France. Meanwhile Sweden looked to France as an ally to hold off Russia. Russia was fast conquering an Asian empire of steppe and forest, but the Russians also wanted a port for trade with western Europe.

Louis XIV ruled France for 72 years, the longest reign in modern European history. His success in building up and strengthening his realm made the rest of Europe envious and fearful. But Louis was extravagant and his wars were costly. He also created fear at home. In the 1680s Protestant refugees fled France, fearing persecution after Louis revoked the Edict of Nantes, which had kept religious peace.

A French trapper and Indians

▼ NEW WORLD, NEW NAMES

In 1613 a shipload of Dutch traders wintered on a small island off the east coast of America. The Indians called the island Manhattan. There the Dutch founded a small colony. They bought the island from the Indians and built a settlement of wooden houses which they called New Amsterdam. But in 1664 English warships sailed into the harbour. England and Holland were at war, and the Dutch governor, Peter Stuyvesant, was forced to surrender the colony. When the war ended, the English renamed the colony New York.

▲ THE FRENCH FUR TRADERS

In the 1600s felt hats became popular in Europe. The best fur for making felt was beaver from North America. French adventurers set off into the wilderness, travelling on foot, and by rafts or canoe down the rivers. They made friends with the Indians, trading knives and other goods for furs. Because French traders explored the Great Lakes and followed the Mississippi river south to the Gulf of Mexico, France claimed much of Canada and the territory drained by the Mississippi and its tributaries.

Settlers in New York

1650–1670

1652 Dutch found first European settlement in South Africa.
1653 End of the Fronde disturbances in France.
1657 Shah Jahan loses Mogul throne to his son Aurangzeb.
1658 Dutch take Ceylon (now Sri Lanka) from Portuguese.
1660 English restore monarchy.
1661 Kang-hsi becomes Emperor of China.
1664 English take over New Amsterdam (New York) from Dutch.
1665 Congolese defeated by Portuguese.
1666 Great Fire of London.
1669 Aurangzeb begins persecution of Hindus.
1670 Hudson's Bay Company founded for Canadian trade.

1670–1700

1670s–80s French explore Great Lakes and Mississippi.
1674 Sivaji leads Marathas against Mogul empire.
1681 Manchus control all of mainland China.
1682 Peter the Great, aged 16, becomes Russia's tsar.
1683 Manchus control Formosa (Taiwan).
1685 Louis XIV cancels Edict of Nantes and persecution of French Protestants begins: Huguenots flee abroad.
1690 England founds trading base at Calcutta in India.
1699 French colonization of Louisiana.
1700 Outbreak of Great Northern War between Sweden and its Baltic neighbours.

Asia and Africa

China's new rulers, the Manchus, ended Ming resistance when they captured the island of Taiwan from the rebels in 1683. The Chinese armies also conquered Mongolia.

In India, Aurangzeb seized the Mogul throne from his father, Shah Jahan (see page 39). Aurangzeb was a tyrant, who was opposed by the Hindu leader Sivaji, chief of the Marathas. From then on, the Mogul Empire started to decline.

In South-East Asia, the Dutch increasingly controlled trade, and this alarmed the king of Siam (today Thailand). He called on French help, but found the French to be as ambitious as the Dutch. But in South Africa the Dutch had no European rivals and established a colony at Cape Town (see page 33).

Plague, fire and revolution

England ended its experiment with republicanism in 1660 when Charles II was restored as King. In 1665 the country suffered an outbreak of bubonic plague which killed more than 75,000 people. The following year, the Great Fire destroyed 13,000 of London's wooden houses (see below). To make matters worse, the Dutch fleet sailed into the River Medway and defeated the English navy.

Charles II was popular, but his brother James II, a convert to Roman Catholicism, was not. In 1688, three years after becoming King, James was deposed. The English found a new King, William III of the Netherlands, a Protestant who had married James's eldest daughter. Following this 'Glorious Revolution' (see page 33), James fled into exile.

Another revolution, with greater impact, had also begun: a revolution in science and commerce. At Cambridge University, the young mathematics professor Isaac Newton was working out why the Universe behaves as it does, why things move as they do, and how sunlight is made up of coloured rays.

▶ LONDON BURNS

On 2 September 1666 fire destroyed a house in London's Pudding Lane, a street of old wooden houses near London Bridge. The blaze swiftly spread, fanned by a strong wind, and burned for four days. Among the buildings burned down was St Paul's Cathedral. Many Londoners fled by boat on the Thames, and only six people died in the fire. From the ashes of medieval London rose some fine new buildings, the most famous of which was the new St Paul's Cathedral, designed by Sir Christopher Wren. It was Wren's greatest achievement.

Londoners fleeing the flames

EUROPE

1650s–60s Plague kills many people in Europe.
1652 England and Holland at war; two more wars follow, ending 1674.
1653 Oliver Cromwell Lord Protector of England.
1654 Abdication of Queen Christina of Sweden.
1660 Charles II restored to throne of England.
1661 Louis XIV absolute monarch of France.
1667 Poland cedes Kiev to Russia.
1668 Spain recognizes independence of Portugal.
1672 Poland at war with Turks and Cossacks; John Sobieski king from 1674.
1682 Peter the Great becomes Tsar of Russia.
1688–89 Glorious Revolution in England deposes James II.
1690 Battle of the Boyne, in Ireland, ends James's hopes of return.
1697 Treaty of Ryswick ends Nine Years' War; France defeated by Grand Alliance.

Dutch visitors to South Africa

⊛ THE DUTCH IN SOUTH AFRICA

The first European to sail around the Cape of Good Hope at the southern tip of Africa was Bartolomeu Dias of Portugal in 1488. By 1600 the Cape was a stopping-off point for European ships sailing to Asia. Crews took on water and traded for food with the local people. In 1652 the Dutch East India Company sent Jan van Riebeeck to the Cape to build a fort and start a vegetable farm. Van Riebeeck needed workers. At first, he had slaves brought in from Asia, but later Dutch freemen started their own farms. In this way the Dutch gained a foothold in South Africa.

James on his way to France

⊛ THE 'GLORIOUS REVOLUTION'

James II became King of England and Scotland in 1685. He favoured Catholicism, though his realm was Protestant, as was his daughter Mary. In 1688 James's second wife gave birth to a son, a possible future Catholic King. Protestant leaders asked Mary's husband, the Dutch prince William of Orange, for aid, and William's army landed in England in November 1689. There was little fighting. James escaped, was recaptured by fishermen and then sailed off to exile in France. William and Mary became joint rulers. The whole episode is known as the 'Glorious Revolution'.

ASIA	AFRICA	AMERICA	THE ARTS
1650 Period of economic growth begins in Japan. **1657** Shah Jahan loses power in India. His sons struggle for succession, and Aurangzeb triumphs. **1661** Kang-hsi becomes Emperor of China; he welcomes Western missionaries. **1662** Koxinga, Chinese rebel, seizes Formosa. **1664** French East India Company founded. Persia opens trade with France. **1669** Hindu religion prohibited in Mogul India. **1674** Sivaji defeats Moguls; Maratha kingdom in west-central India. **1676** Sikh uprisings in India, until 1678. **1683** Koxinga's grandson, Cheng Chin, surrenders Formosa to Manchus. **1689** Russia and China settle borders by Treaty of Nerchinsk. **1690** Founding of Calcutta in India, by English traders. **1697** Chinese occupy Outer Mongolia.	**1650s** The Gold Coast: European countries compete for control of gold and slave trades. **1652** Cape Town settlement founded by Dutch. **1652** English Civil War spreads to Gambia River where English royalists attack republican colony. **1659** French found trading station on coast of Senegal. **1665** Battle of Ambuila; Portuguese destroy Kongo kingdom. **1672** English found Royal African Company, to run slave trade between Morocco and the Cape of Good Hope. **1673** Religious war in western Sahara, begun by Islamic fundamentalists. **1680s–90s** Portuguese lose control of East African strongholds to African and Arab rivals. **1700** Rise of Asante kingdom on the West African Gold Coast.	**1650s** French begin colonization of Canada. **1655** English capture Jamaica from Spain. **1664** English take New Amsterdam from Dutch and change its name to New York. **1670** Hudson's Bay Company founded to encourage English trade in Canada. **1670** By now England has 12 colonies along the eastern coast of North America. **1675** King Philip's War: Indians attack settlers in New England. **1682** Robert Sieur de La Salle of France explores the Great Lakes and Mississippi south to the Gulf of Mexico. **1682** William Penn, English Quaker, founds Pennsylvania colony. **1687** Spain loses Haiti (half of the island of Hispaniola) to France. **1699** French colonization of Louisiana begins.	**1650** Japanese popular literary culture begins: drama, novels, puppet theatre. **1656** The architect Bernini plans a huge piazza in front of St Peter's church in Rome. **1660s** Classical period of French culture: playwrights (Molière, Racine, Corneille); painters Poussin, Claude; composers Lully, Couperin. **1666** Death of Japanese master potter Kakiemon. **1666** Académie Française founded. **1667** John Milton, English poet, publishes his epic poem *Paradise Lost*. **1669** Death of the great Dutch painter Rembrandt. **1678** John Bunyan, English writer, publishes *Pilgrim's Progress*. **1689** Purcell, English composer, writes *Dido and Aeneas*.

INVESTING IN KNOWLEDGE

On 28 November 1660 a group of English scientists founded a new academy of learning. King Charles II gave the group his support and in 1662 the academy became the Royal Society. Among its members were two truly great scientists, Robert Boyle and Isaac Newton. The Society brought together physicists, chemists, astronomers, mathematicians, geographers and many other educated people who simply wanted to know more about the world.

A meeting place for thinkers

At about this time, the first modern banks were being started. People began to realize that knowledge, too, was an investment for the future. Scientists in different countries exchanged ideas in letters. The Society's members shared a belief in experiment –

'see it for yourself' was their motto. They were keen to watch demonstrations of new inventions. The Frenchman Denis Papin showed the Society how his steam pressure cooker softened even the toughest bones.

Science no longer feared the wrath of the Church, which had tried to silence Galileo 50 years earlier (see page 27). Newton was a religious person, yet he was not afraid of

▽ At a meeting of the Royal Society, Denis Papin showed the members the world's first pressure cooker. Papin was French and came to London in 1665 to work with the physicist Robert Boyle. This 'steam digester' demonstrated the power of high-pressure steam.

1640–1665

1642 Blaise Pascal in France makes an adding machine, with geared wheels.
1643 Evangelista Torricelli in Italy invents the mercury barometer.
1647 Otto von Guericke in Germany invents air pump.
1650s Study of gases; Van Helmont of Belgium probably the first to use the term 'gas'.
1657 Christiaan Huygens of Holland makes the first accurate clock, with a swinging pendulum.
1658 Jan Swannerdam of Holland is first to observe red blood cells.
1662 Robert Boyle formulates gas laws.

putting forward startling new ideas. Others too, such as the Dutchman Antonie van Leeuwenhoek, who developed the first powerful microscope, were breaking new ground. Everywhere science was growing in confidence. The astronomer Edmund Halley even predicted that a comet (now named after him) seen in 1682 would return in 1758 – and it did.

1665–1675

1665 Robert Hooke publishes *Micrographia*, a book with the first drawings of plant cells.
1665 Pierre de Fermat, French mathematician, dies. He helped develop modern number theory.
1665 Isaac Newton uses glass prisms to show the nature of light.
1669 Newton makes the first reflecting telescope.
1670s Antonie van Leeuwenhoek in Holland uses a microscope to study microbes.
1673 Gottfried von Leibnitz, a German mathematician, improves on Pascal's calculator to make it multiply and divide.

1675–1700

1675 Royal Greenwich Observatory is founded in England.
1676 Leibnitz invents the calculus, a form of mathematics also invented independently by Newton and by Kowa Seki of Japan.
1678 Edmund Halley in England publishes catalogue of stars in the southern hemisphere.
1679 Robert Hooke invents the balance spring.
1687 Newton publishes *Principia Mathematica* ('Mathematical Principles').
1690 Huygens suggests that light is made up of waves.

▽ French scientist Blaise Pascal with a mercury barometer on the tower of St Jacques-la-Boucherie, Paris. He showed that air pressure falls with an increase in altitude.

△ The microscope was invented in the late 1500s. By the mid 1600s Antonie van Leeuwenhoek was making powerful microscopes able to reveal minute bacteria.

DESPOTS AND DEMOCRATS

When a king or queen died childless, the absence of a natural heir was always a likely cause of trouble. Usually there were several claimants to a vacant throne, because members of royal families of different countries often married each other. Each claimant attracted powerful backing from states who were anxious to gain diplomatic or territorial advantage by giving their support.

In 1701 a war broke out in Europe over who should rule Spain. The childless Charles II of Spain had offered the throne to Philip of France, grandson of Louis XIV. At first Louis refused to support the move, but temptation proved too great, and he agreed. However, the Protestants were strongly opposed, fearing that France and Spain might unite.

Quarrels over succession

The War of the Spanish Succession lasted until 1713. The French were outfought by the armies of the Duke of Marlborough and Prince Eugene of Savoy, and the British navy captured Gibraltar from Spain. In the end, Louis XIV got his way: Philip became the king of Spain, but it was agreed that France and Spain would separate. The war cost France dearly. Prices and taxes rose, and there were revolts against the government.

In 1702, England's last Stuart monarch, Queen Anne, came to the throne. After Anne died, there was again a disputed succession. George, Elector of Hanover in Germany, was the great-grandson of James I. James Edward Stuart was the son of the deposed James II.

▼ THE SOUTH SEA BUBBLE

Since the founding of the Bank of England in 1694, London had grown as a financial centre. In 1711 Queen Anne's government encouraged the setting up of the South Sea Company. People bought stock, hoping to profit from the Company's trade with South America. The price of stock rose, and more people rushed to buy. They sold houses and land in order to purchase pieces of paper promising shares in all kinds of fanciful money-making schemes. In 1720 the 'bubble' of speculation burst. South Sea stock was worthless and many people were ruined. Britain's prime minister, Robert Walpole, was empowered to sort things out.

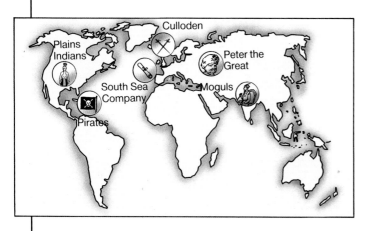

Keeping Company records

△ Some European nations moved slowly towards parliamentary government and a modern trade and money-market system. But scandal such as the South Sea Bubble, and rebellion caused confusion and uncertainty. In North America the eastern colonies thrived, the western Indians still roamed their hunting grounds. Piracy and smuggling flourished around the coasts of America.

1700–1725

1700 Asante power grows in West Africa.
1700–21 Great Northern War between Sweden and Russia, Denmark and Poland.
1701–13 War of Spanish Succession.
1707 Union of England and Scotland.
1712 St Petersburg is new capital of Russian Empire.
1715 Death of Louis XIV, King of France.
1722 Death of Kang-hsi, Chinese emperor.
1723 China at war with Mongols.
1724 Russians and Turks agree to divide Persia between them.

1725–1750

1730 Rise of Marathas in India.
1733 Family pact between Bourbons of France and Spain.
1733 Georgia is last of Britain's 13 colonies in North America.
1733 War of Polish Succession.
1738 Nadir Shah of Persia invades India.
1740 War of Austrian Succession.
1740s Beginning of British–French rivalry in India.
1745 Start of last Jacobite rebellion in Britain.
1748 Treaty of Aix-la-Chapelle ends War of Austrian Succession.

The battle of Culloden

◉ JACOBITE UPRISINGS

James II, England's last Catholic king, died in exile in 1701. His supporters were known as Jacobites, from the Latin word for James, *Jacobus*. They swore loyalty to James's son James Edward Stuart. In 1715 Jacobites rose in rebellion against George I, but failed. The Stuart cause lived on in Scotland where, in 1745, Highland clansmen rallied to Charles Edward Stuart, James Edward's son, known as 'Bonnie Prince Charlie'. The rebels invaded England but gained no support. The Highlanders were finally defeated at Culloden Moor in 1746, and Charles fled into exile.

Ministers and rulers

George I, a Protestant, became King in 1714. A foreigner in his new kingdom, George relied heavily on his government, headed from 1721 to 1742 by the able Sir Robert Walpole. Walpole was the King's 'prime' minister, meaning the first or most important minister, who led government meetings. George, who spoke no English, took no part in them.

Walpole had to fend off a rebellion by Stuart supporters (see above) and restore people's confidence in the economy. Britain's growing trade was international, with America and India as well as Europe. Banking and finance were developing, but no one really understood how the economic system worked. A financial crash like the South Sea Bubble (see page 36) not only ruined investors, it also caused deeper unease.

In Russia the new tsar, Peter the Great, who ruled from 1689 to 1725, was anxious to modernize his own country along Western lines. He visited western Europe in disguise. He was impressed with Louis XIV's absolute power and with Britain's naval dockyards. Peter later went to war with Sweden, and despite the military skill of the Swedish king Charles XII, Russia was too strong for him. In 1714 the tsar moved to his newly-built capital, St Petersburg. Under Peter, Russia became a European power (see right).

◉ PETER THE GREAT'S RUSSIA

When Peter the Great, Tsar of Russia, visited England in 1698, his hosts thought that all Russians were barbarians. The tsar and his companions drank heavily and smashed furniture. But Peter's trip to the West had a serious purpose. He inspected factories, shipyards and armouries. He wanted to know how government and taxation worked. Back in Russia, Peter was powerful enough to enforce changes, even making nobles cut off their beards so that they looked more 'European'. When Peter died in 1725, Russia had gained new seaports in wars against Sweden and Persia, and its empire stretched from the Baltic to the Pacific.

Peter the Great inspecting a dockyard

Trade and warfare

The early 1700s were a time of growth in both East and West. China prospered under strong Manchu emperors, who increased their empire by military conquest. But as China's population swelled to over 300 million, there were food shortages that led to peasant riots. Europeans were keen to buy Chinese tea and porcelain, but frustrated by China's refusal to accept any Western goods, except silver, in return.

Wars could increase trade, both legal and illegal. In 1739 Britain, urged on by its merchants and landowners, went to war with Spain. Ships trading with America were easy prey for pirates based on the islands of the Caribbean and South America (see right). In central Europe it was monarchs, not merchants, who called for war. Prussia was now a strong military power, rivalling Austria, and wanted to prove it.

Blackbeard meets his end

◉ MARAUDING PIRATES

The Caribbean Sea was dangerous for merchant ships. There was every chance of an attack by pirates, also known as buccaneers. Buccaneers seized goods from merchant ships and sold them to the Spanish colonies, who were banned from foreign trade. Madagascar in the Indian Ocean was also a favourite pirate haunt – an ideal base for raids on ships voyaging to the East Indies. Edward Teach, nicknamed Blackbeard, was a well-known ruthless English pirate. In 1718 he was killed at sea by sailors sent by the governor of Virginia, an English colony.

▼ PLAINS HUNTERS

Until the Spaniards arrived in America in the 1500s, the Indians had no horses. The native horses of the New World had died out long before, but the Indians caught and tamed wild descendants of Spanish horses. The horse was particularly important to the Plains Indians of the prairie, such as the Sioux, Cheyenne and Comanche. They fought and hunted on horseback, and a chief counted his wealth in horses. The Indians hunted buffalo, which roamed in herds numbering millions, for meat and hides. Before the 1800s few people apart from native Americans had ventured into the territory of the Plains Indians.

An Indian village

EUROPE

1701 Act of Settlement bars Roman Catholic Stuarts from British throne.
1709 Battle of Poltava: Russians defeat Swedes.
1714 George the Elector of Hanover becomes George I of Britain.
1715 Death of Louis XIV of France.
1720 South Sea Bubble financial crisis.
1721 Robert Walpole Britain's first prime minister.
1725 Death of Peter the Great of Russia.
1733–35 War of Polish Succession: Russia and Austria triumph over France and Sweden.
1739–41 War of Jenkins' Ear between Spain and Britain.
1740 Outbreak of War of Austrian Succession: Frederick the Great attacks Austrian Silesia.
1745–46 Charles Stuart leads Jacobite rebellion; Scots beaten at Culloden.
1748 End of War of Austrian Succession; Prussia keeps Silesia.

Aurangzeb, the tyrant

⏾ LAST OF THE MOGULS

Aurangzeb (1618–1707) was the last of the great Mogul emperors of India. He was a devout Muslim, who scorned the pursuit of pleasure. Aurangzeb wanted only power. He seized the throne in 1659, imprisoning his sick father and ruthlessly ordering the deaths of his brothers. At first he ruled well, but he later turned against the Hindus, who had previously served the Muslim emperors willingly. He fought wars in southern India against the rebellious Marathas and also against the Sikhs. These wars seriously weakened the Mogul Empire.

The War of the Austrian Succession

In 1740 Austria gained a new ruler, the Empress Maria Theresa. Her succession was the signal for conflict. Frederick of Prussia decided that now was the time to test Austrian strength and went to war, backed by France. Once again, other nations joined in to grab what they could. Russia fought its old enemy, Sweden. Britain sided with Austria, against France. The war ended in 1748, and Maria Theresa kept her throne.

Britain and France were also rivals for trade in India, where the Mogul Empire was weakening (see left), and they opposed each other in North America. There Britain had more settlers but France claimed the larger territory. Rivalry led to some fighting in the east, where most European settlers lived. To Europeans, the great western plains and mountains were still a wilderness, roamed by Plains Indians (see page 38).

ASIA

1707 Aurangzeb, Mogul emperor of India, dies and the empire begins to decline.
1709 Afghans revolt against Persian rule.
1720 Chinese send troops to set up garrisons in Tibet.
1721 Edo (Tokyo) in Japan is probably the largest city in the world, with about 800,000 inhabitants.
1722 Death of the Chinese emperor Kang-hsi, after a 61-year reign.
1723–35 China at war with the Mongols.
1730s Marathas are the most powerful force in India.
1736 In Persia, Nadir Shah overthrows the Safavid dynasty.
1739 Turkey gains Serbia from Austria.
1747 Kingdom of Afghanistan is founded.
1747 Nadir Shah of Persia is assassinated.
1748 English recapture Madras in India from the French.

AFRICA, PACIFIC

1712 Asante king Osei Tutu killed by enemies. (He led the Asante to dominance, trading with the Dutch from his capital, Kumasi.)
1713 South Africa: smallpox epidemic weakens Khoikoin tribes in Cape Colony, and their resistance to Dutch settlement fades.
1725 Vitus Bering, a Dane, explores the eastern Pacific for Russia, and navigates the strait separating Alaska and Siberia (the Bering Strait).
1730 Portuguese lose control of Mombasa in East Africa.
1731 Oyo (Yoruba) Empire in West Africa defeats its neighbour Dahomey after 50 years of war.
1750 Asante Empire now controls all the Gold Coast (today Ghana and neighbouring states).
1750 Egypt, part of the Ottoman Empire, in confusion as Ottoman rulers and Mameluke beys (regional governors) contest control.

AMERICA

1702–13 Queen Anne's War; France and Spain against Britain with American Indian allies.
1704 First successful American newspaper, *The Boston News-Letter.*
1712 Carolina divided into North and South Carolinas.
1713 Britain wins contract to sell slaves from Africa to Spanish settlements in America.
1732 George Washington born in Virginia.
1733 Foundation of Georgia colony, last of the 13 British colonies in North America.
1739 Pierre and Paul Malet, French explorers, journey across the Great Plains and sight the Rocky Mountains.
1742 Peruvian Indians revolt against Spain.
1744 King George's War, fought between Britain and France in North America.
1750 Portugal and Spain sign an agreement fixing areas of rule in South America.

SCIENCE, SOCIETY

1701 Jethro Tull invents a seed drill, a machine for sowing seeds in rows.
1712 Last execution in Britain of a person charged with witchcraft.
1712 Thomas Newcomen (Britain) designs a steam pumping engine.
1714 Fahrenheit (Germany) invents mercury thermometer.
1719 Daniel Defoe publishes *Robinson Crusoe*, a novel based on a real-life experience.
1720 Last outbreak of plague in Europe, in southern France.
1726 Jonathan Swift publishes satirical novel *Gulliver's Travels.*
1730 Methodism founded by John and Charles Wesley.
1733 In Britain John Kay invents the flying shuttle, to speed up weaving.
1735 John Harrison (Britain) invents the marine chronometer, a clock that keeps accurate time at sea, essential for navigation.

THE SUN KING

In 1661, Cardinal Mazarin, the adviser to King Louis XIV, died. Louis, then aged 22, told his ministers that, from that time on, they should obey only their king. Louis firmly believed that God had chosen him as France's ruler, who could do no wrong. For the rest of his long reign, until 1715, the king's word alone was law.

An all-powerful king needed suitably impressive homes, so Louis began a vast building programme. By far the most extravagant of his new palaces was Versailles, built on the site of his father's hunting lodge. No expense was spared in its construction. Louis cared only for the grandeur of France and his own greater glory. The well-being of ordinary people did not interest the king.

Louis was famed as the most splendid monarch in Europe, the 'Sun King'. But he was also feared as an aggressor, who took France into expensive wars and demanded large armies to fight them. By the 1690s one in four Frenchmen was under arms.

In 1682 Louis was ready to move into his magnificent palace of Versailles. It was the largest royal residence in Europe, lavishly furnished and decorated, and surrounded by splendid gardens. Versailles took 1,500 servants to look after it.

▽ At Versailles, King Louis XIV loved lavish entertainments such as masques (plays with music and dance). He approved the elaborate costume designs, just as he authorized everything else that went on at Versailles. Courtiers were expected to attend the king every day, or risk his displeasure.

FRANCE'S 'SUN KING'

1661 Louis XIV decides to be his own first (prime) minister and rule absolutely.
1683 Death of Jean Baptiste Colbert, France's finance minister, who encouraged commerce and spent money on new roads and canals.
1685 Persecution of the Protestant Huguenots begins.
1689 King William's War, the first war in North America fought between France and England.
1704 Battle of Blenheim: French and Bavarians defeated by Allies led by Duke of Marlborough and Prince Eugene of Savoy. France's defeat changes the course of War of Spanish Succession.
1709 Poll tax imposed to pay for France's huge army.
1715 Louis XIV dies, after 72 years as king. He is succeeded by his great-grandson, Louis XV. Until he comes of age at 13 (1723) France is ruled by the Regent, the Duke of Orleans.
1720 Financial scandal in Paris. The new India Company collapses, many people are ruined.
1748 End of War of Austrian Succession: France has to give up the Austrian Netherlands.

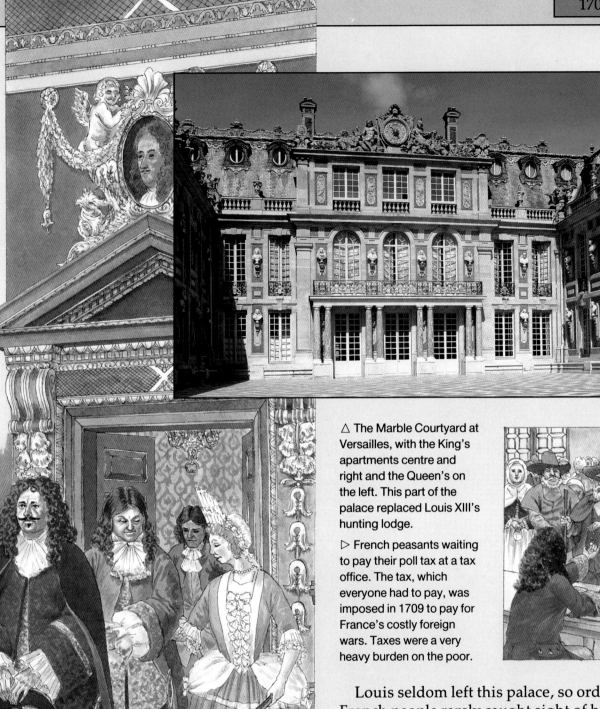

△ The Marble Courtyard at Versailles, with the King's apartments centre and right and the Queen's on the left. This part of the palace replaced Louis XIII's hunting lodge.

▷ French peasants waiting to pay their poll tax at a tax office. The tax, which everyone had to pay, was imposed in 1709 to pay for France's costly foreign wars. Taxes were a very heavy burden on the poor.

Louis seldom left this palace, so ordinary French people rarely caught sight of him. His nobles passed their time at court, flattering the king's vanity to win royal favour. They followed Louis everywhere: to the royal Mass, to the royal hunt and to evening entertainments. This enabled Louis to keep an eye on them and make sure that they were not plotting against him or each other. But for many nobles, and France, the cost of all this was crippling.

THE WORLD EXPANDS

After the failure of the last Stuart rebellion in 1745 (see page 37), Britain was in a stronger position to challenge France for colonial supremacy. France was still living on memories of past glories. Britain, by contrast, had a flourishing economy, a fairer system of government and a strong navy.

The war for America

In North America fur trappers and settlers from the British colonies began moving west, across the Ohio river and into territory claimed by France. In 1754 war broke out. Young George Washington from Virginia volunteered with other colonists to help British troops fight the French.

The French and Indian War took place in the forests and mountains (see below right). British troops, unused to fighting in these conditions, suffered defeat after defeat.

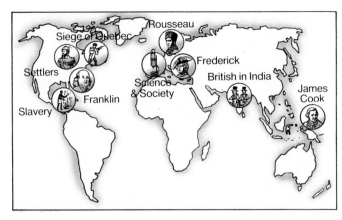

△ France and Britain strove for supremacy in North America and India. New scientific and philosophical ideas abounded in Europe and America.

Indians spy on British troops

⦿ FRENCH AND INDIAN WAR

From the 1600s until 1763 France and England fought for control of North America. They both claimed territory belonging to the Indians and encouraged Indian tribes to fight on their side. In 1754 the French built forts to stop settlers from Britain's colonies moving westward into land claimed by France. This move was seen as an act of aggression and a signal for war. Virginian colonists led by George Washington attacked the French, but were driven back. British troops sent to help the colonists were ill-equipped for fighting in forests. Their red uniforms made them easy targets for an enemy ambush.

1750–1760	1760–1770
1750 Britain's Industrial Revolution speeds up. In art and architecture, Neoclassical styles become popular instead of decorative Baroque and Rococo. **1751** First volume of Diderot's Encyclopedia is published in France. **1754** French and Indian War in North America. **1755** Lisbon destroyed by earthquake. **1756** Seven Years' War starts: mainly Prussia against Austria and Russia in Europe; Britain against France for empires. **1756** Wolfgang Amadeus Mozart, Austrian composer, born. **1757** Battle of Plassey in India: Britain gains control of Bengal. **1759** Pombal, Portugal's prime minister, introduces reforms. **1760** British conquer French Canada. **1760** George III becomes King of Great Britain.	**1760** Enclosure Act in Britain: change in farming methods. **1762** Rousseau, French philosopher, publishes *The Social Contract*. **1762** Catherine the Great becomes ruler of Russia. **1763** Seven Years' War ended by the Treaty of Paris. **1766** Louis de Bougainville of France sets sail on round-the-world voyage. **1766** Henry Cavendish discovers hydrogen gas. **1767** Mason–Dixon line separates slave-owning colonies from 'free' colonies in North America. **1767** Burmese capture capital of Siam. **1768** Captain Cook begins his first voyage to chart the Pacific. **1770** British troops fire on crowd in Boston. **1770** Cook lands in New South Wales, Australia. **1770** Russians destroy Ottoman fleet in Mediterranean.

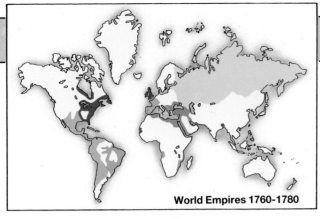

World Empires 1760-1780

☐ Spanish
☐ Portuguese
☐ Dutch
☐ British
☐ French
☐ Russian
☐ Ottoman

△ The main European colonies in the late 1700s. Britain was gaining a growing empire, largely at the expense of France.

The war in America was soon overtaken by a larger European conflict, the Seven Years' War (1756–63). This was really two wars. One was a land campaign in Europe fought between the Prussian army and the armies of Austria, Russia and France. The other was a sea and land war fought between Britain and France over colonies.

▼ THE FALL OF CANADA

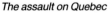

In 1759 General James Wolfe, at the head of British troops, launched an attack from the St Lawrence River in a bid to seize Quebec from the French. British soldiers climbed steep cliffs, overpowered the few French guards and formed up on the Heights of Abraham. The French commander Montcalm had no choice but to attack. Both he and Wolfe were killed in the battle, which was won by the British. The following year, Britain captured Montreal. The Treaty of Paris, which ended the Seven Years' War, also ended France's ambitions of an American empire.

The assault on Quebec

In Europe, Britain supported Prussia with money. In the colonial war, Prime Minister Pitt sent fresh troops to North America with new commanders to lead them. The young General Wolfe defeated the French at Quebec in 1759 and within a year all of Canada was under British rule (see below left). The American colonists had helped in this victory and now wanted more say in their own affairs (see below).

Clive in India

In Asia, the richest colonial prize was India. Mogul rule had collapsed. There was still an emperor in Delhi, but he was powerless. French and British trading companies supported rival Indian rulers in local wars and competed for influence. Britain emerged victorious, thanks to Robert Clive of the British East India Company.

▼ FRANKLIN'S AMERICA

Americans were used to doing things for themselves. No one demonstrated this more brilliantly than Benjamin Franklin, who was born in 1706 in Boston. Franklin spent only two years at school but taught himself a great deal from books. He became a printer and newspaper publisher in Philadelphia, where he served as postmaster, started a library and did much to improve the city. He invented an efficient stove, bifocal eyeglasses and the lightning conductor. He served as a diplomat in London and Paris and helped draw up the Declaration of Independence.

Franklin the printer

◉ THE BRITISH IN INDIA

With the decline of the Moguls in India, a new empire gradually arose. Its builders were British merchants based in Calcutta and Madras who worked for the East India Company. The Company had a small army of British and Indian troops, and a lot of gold to hand out to friendly Indian rulers. In 1756 the Nawab of Bengal seized Calcutta. Britons were captured and imprisoned in a storeroom, which became known as the 'Black Hole'. The Nawab was defeated by Company troops led by Robert Clive at the battle of Plassey in 1757.

△ Officials of the British East India Company taking tea. By 1763 it controlled much of India.

Colonies in India

Lucknow
INDIA
Calcutta
Bombay
GOA
■ British
● Madras
□ Portuguese
CEYLON

(see above)

EUROPE

1752 Britain adopts the Gregorian calendar.
1756 Prussia invades Saxony, starting the Seven Years' War: Britain, Hanover, Prussia fight Austria, Russia, France, Sweden.
1756 William Pitt becomes Britain's prime minister.
1760 George II of Britain dies; his grandson George III becomes king.
1760 Berlin is burned by Russian and Austrian armies.
1762 Britain and Spain at war.
1762 Catherine the Great replaces her husband Peter III as Russian ruler.
1763 Treaty of Paris ends Seven Years' War.
1764 Stanislas Poniatowski becomes King of Poland.
1765 Joseph II emperor of Austria.
1767 Catherine the Great plans reforms in Russia.
1770 Johann Struensee is effectively ruler of Sweden, in place of the ailing king Christian VII.

The battle of Plassey assured the East India Company control of the rich province of Bengal. This was the foundation for Britain's Indian Empire (see above).

The Seven Years' War was a triumph for Britain, and particularly for the British navy. In Europe, Prussia was exhausted, despite Frederick the Great's military prowess. France was ruined, and its economy was crumbling. It had lost both an empire in Canada and its trading position in India.

Farther shores

The Pacific Ocean was still largely unexplored. The Chinese and Japanese knew its western fringes, but had not sailed across it. Voyagers from South America had sailed west, to Easter Island, and the Maoris had come in canoes from Polynesia to New Zealand, 'land of the long white cloud'.

▼ COOK'S FIRST VOYAGE

Captain James Cook left Britain in September 1768 in the converted coal-ship *Endeavour*. On board were 94 people and stores to last them for 18 months. Cook himself chose the diet, which included concentrated soup and lemon juice, to help prevent the terrible disease scurvy. The *Endeavour* sailed first to Tahiti in the Pacific Ocean, where scientists made astronomical observations, and then round New Zealand, before heading west to Australia to explore the dangerous Great Barrier Reef. Cook brought his ship safely home in July 1771.

The Endeavour *in Tahiti*

ASIA	AFRICA	AMERICA	PACIFIC
1750 Tibetans rebel against Chinese rule. **1751** French fail to capture Arcot from British after siege. **1751** Japanese shogun Tokugawa Yoshimune, a man of humble lifestyle, dies. **1752** Afghans capture Lahore (now in Pakistan). **1754** Skilful French governor Joseph Dupleix recalled from India. **1755** Burmese found new capital at Rangoon. **1756** Black Hole of Calcutta: Siraj-ud-Dowla imprisons 146 British residents in a small storehouse. Most die. **1757** Battle of Plassey: Clive overthrows Siraj-ud-Dowla and takes control of Bengal for Britain. **1761** Battle of Panipat: Afghans defeat Mogul emperor and his Maratha allies. Moguls now unable to resist foreign rule. **1767** Turkey at war with Russia, until 1774.	**1752** War in Sudan: the sultan of Darfur dies in battle against the armies of Kordofan. **1755** Outbreak of smallpox (brought by European settlers) around the Cape of Good Hope kills many Africans. **1756** The ruler of Algiers seizes Tunis. **1757** Mulay Muhammad, Morocco's new ruler, brings in reforms. **1760s** West Africa increasingly under Islamic influence. North Africa and much of East Africa are ruled by Muslims.	**1754–60** French and Indian War. **1759** French lose Quebec to British, led by Wolfe. **1760** French surrender Montreal to Britain, **1762** France cedes to Spain all its lands west of the Mississippi. **1763** British declare land west of the Allegheny Mountains to be Indian reserve. **1763** Chief Pontiac leads Indian uprising in Great Lakes region. **1763** Charles Mason and Jeremiah Dixon begin their boundary survey. **1763** Rio de Janeiro becomes capital of Brazil. **1764** French set up trading post at St Louis. **1765** Britain imposes Stamp Act on printed matter. **1765** First British colony in Falkland Islands. France already has a settlement there. **1766** Britain repeals the Stamp Act. **1770** 'Boston Massacre'.	**1766** Samuel Wallis (Britain) sails round the world; he discovers the Society Islands (Tahiti). **1766** Louis de Bougainville sets sail from France to explore Pacific. He visits Tahiti and Samoa but does not sight Australia. **1768** Cook leaves Britain in the Royal Navy ship *Endeavour*. **1769** Bougainville returns to France, having visited the East Indies on the way. **1769** Cook explores New Zealand, making the first accurate map of both islands and meeting the Maoris, who are unfriendly. **1769** Jean-François de Surville of France visits New Zealand and quarrels with Maoris. **1770** Cook sights the east coast of Australia. His crew land at Botany Bay and Cook claims New South Wales for Britain, describing it as a suitable territory for settlement.

▼ SLAVERY IN THE NEW WORLD

From America's plantations came Europe's cotton, sugar and tobacco. The plantation workers were almost all slaves. Most of those who survived the voyage from Africa endured a life, often pitifully short, of hard work and brutality. On a Caribbean island sugar plantation at harvest time, slaves worked from dawn till dusk, cutting cane and carrying it to the mills for processing. Overseers controlled the slaves with whips, and any who ran away were cruelly punished. The slaves preserved memories of their African homeland in their music and songs, which they often chanted in unison.

Slaves cutting sugar cane

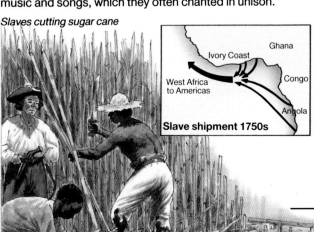

In the 18th century the greatest navigator of the Pacific was possibly Britain's James Cook (see page 44). On the first of three epic voyages, he visited Tahiti, New Zealand and Australia. The French explorer Bougainville circled the world in the 1760s, visiting Tahiti and New Guinea.

Stirrings of conscience

Many Europeans were fascinated by accounts of people whom they called 'savages' in faraway lands (see page 46). The Tahitians of the South Pacific, for example, seemed to dwell in an earthly paradise, where work and daily worries were unknown. Very different was the misery of the thousands of black slaves who worked the plantations in America and the West Indies. In Europe and America, many people declared that slavery was wrong and called for its abolition.

45

▼ THE 'NOBLE SAVAGE'

Lee Boo, a Pacific islander, was a guest celebrity at parties in London in the 1780s. He was shown off, dressed in Western clothes and taken to see the sights. Europeans believed that most people from America, Africa, Asia and the Pacific were 'savages', and that Europe had a duty to 'civilize' them by teaching them Christianity and Western ways. However, the French philosopher Jean-Jacques Rousseau admired such people and believed that Europe could learn much from their way of life.

△ Jean-Jacques Rousseau, author of *The Social Contract*.

▼ SOCIAL AND SCIENTIFIC LIFE

Science was becoming fashionable. In England Joseph Priestley discovered carbon dioxide, and later oxygen. Like many artists and scientists, Priestley had a wealthy aristocratic employer, or patron. The new science was based on experiment in laboratories, which were usually paid for by the patron. The rich enjoyed elegant houses with fine furniture, had paintings by Gainsborough and Canaletto, and listened to music by Haydn and the boy-genius Mozart. Leading writers of the time included Goethe in Germany, and in England Samuel Johnson.

Experimenting with gases

The age of enlightenment

A growing number of people in Europe now believed in 'enlightenment', that is improving conditions through education and reform. But such ideas made little headway in Spanish-ruled South America, or in China and Japan, which were still untouched by Western culture. European idealists looked forward to a better world, where all people could be equal. Above all, they were inspired by the idea of the 'noble savage' (see left). They wondered how people who had no recognizable religion or law seemed happy. By comparison, Europe appeared corrupt.

As the influence of the Church declined in the Western world, so new ideas began to take shape. In London and Paris people in high society, both men and women, mixed with radicals and freethinkers, people who challenged existing beliefs. In America, thinkers were also men of affairs – like Benjamin Franklin and Thomas Jefferson – who were interested in the arts and business as well as science and politics. France, in particular, was buzzing with ideas, but its weak king and inefficient government stood in the way of progress.

SCIENCE

1750s Instrument-making develops in Europe and the American colonies.
1751 John Burton suggests that greater hygiene and care in childbirth would reduce number of deaths.
1752 Benjamin Franklin demonstrates that lightning is a form of electricity.
1762 Death of Lady Mary Wortley Montagu, who introduced inoculation against smallpox to England.
1766 Henry Cavendish, British scientist, discovers the gas hydrogen.
1768 John Hunter pioneers modern surgery.
1769 Nicolas Cugnot of France builds the first steam-powered vehicle.

ARTS

1750s Neoclassical art and portrait painting are fashionable: Gainsborough in England.
1751 First volume of Diderot's Encyclopedia.
1754 Britain's Royal Society of Arts is founded.
1755 Samuel Johnson publishes his Dictionary of the English Language.
1759 Voltaire, French writer, publishes his satire *Candide*.
1762 Rousseau, French philosopher, publishes *The Social Contract*.
1764 Voltaire's *Philosophical Dictionary*.
1770 Births of William Wordsworth, English Romantic writer, and Ludwig van Beethoven, German composer.

Knowledge, freedom and revolution

Russia opened its first university, in Moscow, in 1755, the year that Samuel Johnson published his celebrated English dictionary. Four years earlier, in France, Denis Diderot published the first volume of his great encyclopedia, and the French thinker Voltaire began his association with Frederick the Great, ruler of Prussia (see below). Learning was no longer for the privileged few. More people could now read and write, and from 1759 Londoners were able to visit the newly founded British Museum.

In 1762 the French philosopher Jean-Jacques Rousseau published a book called *The Social Contract*. It begins with the stirring words, 'Man is born free, yet everywhere he is in chains'. In America and France this idea was taken up eagerly by those who wanted change. They believed that everyone should be equal before the law, no one should suffer for their religious beliefs, and people should have more say in government.

In Britain, in 1763, John Wilkes, a Member of Parliament (MP) attacked King George III in a magazine article. He was arrested, but claimed that as an MP he could not be brought to trial. Londoners rioted in support of Wilkes, whose defiance of the King and government made him a hero for budding revolutionaries in Britain and America.

Other revolutions were already underway in Britain: in the fields, along the new canals, in glowing ironworks and in dust-choked coalmines (see pages 48–49). In France, in 1769, a strange road accident was a sign of things to come. An army engineer named Nicolas-Joseph Cugnot drove a hissing, self-propelled steam carriage into a wall. He had built and crashed the first automobile.

▶ FREDERICK AND VOLTAIRE

Frederick the Great of Prussia, who reigned from 1740 to 1786, was in his lifetime Europe's most famous king. A formidable general, he was also a tireless administrator, reorganizing industry, modernizing farming and starting state schools for all. He was an 'enlightened despot': his word was law, but he called himself 'the first servant of the state'. He believed that his country should be ruled well and tolerantly. An admirer of all things French, Frederick struck up an unlikely friendship with the French writer Voltaire, himself no friend of all-powerful kings. They discussed kingship, government and democracy. The friendship ended after they quarrelled over the treatment of a German philosopher by the Prussian Academy.

◁ In Europe, the Seven Years' War was fought in a series of land battles between Prussia and its chief enemies, Austria and Russia. Frederick the Great directed his armies skilfully. Prussia emerged as a European power.

Frederick and Voltaire

INDUSTRY AND FARMING

Britons led the way in the Industrial Revolution, using coke to smelt iron and building the first iron bridge. In 1733 John Kay, a Lancashire man, invented his 'flying' shuttle, to speed up the weaving of cloth. Weavers now needed more spun yarn, so new spinning machines were invented. By 1785 there were power looms, at first driven by water, but later steam-driven. People left their villages and flocked to the towns to find work in the factories. The towns grew rapidly, and between them, canals were dug and roads were built to carry goods.

Farming

Old open fields disappeared, as farmers enclosed their land with hedges. They began to use machinery, such as seed drills, and developed larger breeds of cattle, pigs and sheep. Two new crops, turnips and clover, were introduced. Turnips fed cattle through the winter; clover put nitrogen back into the soil. A new four-year rotation of crops planted in turn meant that fields no longer had to be left fallow (unused) for a year. This enabled farmers to produce more food for the growing population.

RISE OF INDUSTRY

1750s Production of iron in Britain boosted by Darby process for coke-smelting.
1760 Josiah Wedgwood starts a pottery factory in Staffordshire, England.
1761 Duke of Bridgewater's Canal in England, to carry coal.
1765 British imports of cotton increase to supply textile factories.
1763–4 Watt makes his first steam engine, used for pumping.
1764 James Hargreaves invents spinning jenny, for faster spinning.
1769 Richard Arkwright of Britain develops a water-powered spinning frame.
1770s France begins to industrialize slowly. Frederick the Great of Prussia encourages factories and new crops such as sugar beet.

◁ A farmer with an 'improved' bull – much bigger than older breeds. Most agricultural reformers were wealthy landowners. Thomas William Coke and his Norfolk neighbour Viscount Townshend pioneered the new four-year rotation of crops, planting clover in the fourth year to restore nitrogen, and grazing animals on the clover so their manure could increase soil fertility.

Industrial Europe late 1700s

BRITAIN
HOLLAND
London
GERMANY
FRANCE
AUSTRIA-HUNGARY
ITALY

Intensive industry
Limited industry

△ The Industrial Revolution began in England. Other European countries, such as France and Germany, were less ready for it. In the 1700s the first textile factories had machines driven by water power. Hand weavers lost their livelihoods. Stagecoaches rattled along the rough dirt roads. Canals were built to carry heavy materials such as coal. There were no steam railways, but horse-drawn wagons on rails were used around coal mines. Steam pumps drew up water from the mine tunnels.

CHANGING THE OLD ORDER

In 1770 ships of the Russian navy made their first appearance in the Mediterranean and defeated a Turkish fleet. It was a sign of changing times. The Ottoman Empire was weakening while Russia advanced. Poland, Russia's old enemy, would soon vanish from the map as a country in its own right.

Europe had become powerful through trade. Britain and France had tripled their overseas trade since 1700. Silver from Spanish South America was sold across Europe into Asia. Tea, silk and porcelain from China were shipped to Europe.

Society was changing, too, but governments clung to the past. Most countries still ran their affairs in an old-fashioned way. Taxation was in a muddle. Public education and health care hardly existed. Poverty and injustice were everywhere. If there was to be progress, argued the reformers, changes had to be made to bring a greater degree of equality and freedom to all.

Autocrats and democrats

The idea of democracy – government by the people for the people – was still new to Europe. Some autocratic rulers, those with sole power, such as Catherine the Great of Russia, Joseph II of Austria and Frederick the Great of Prussia, welcomed certain aspects of 'enlightenment', but not others. They wanted their countries to run more efficiently, but had no intention of sharing power with the people.

▼ TAKING TO THE AIR

On 21 November 1783 a huge crowd gathered in Paris. They had come to see an historic event: the first flight by people in a balloon. Earlier that year the inventors Joseph and Etienne Montgolfier had sent up animals to show that a hot-air balloon could fly. The next step was a flight by human passengers, the two volunteers Pilâtre de Rozier and the Marquis d'Arlandes. The crowd gasped, then cheered wildly as the balloon rose into the sky. The men on board waved to the crowd below and, after 25 minutes floating above the city, landed to a heroes' welcome.

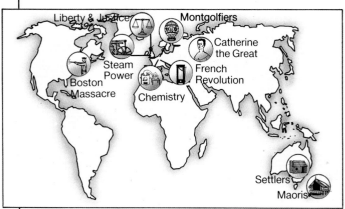

△ As the 1700s drew towards a close, the world was undergoing a period of great changes – scientific, social and political. People took to the skies, the steam engine thundered, and in America and France new systems of government were being shaped by revolution. It was an age of 'enlightened' despots, such as Catherine of Russia, but power was moving away from monarchs to the masses. In the Pacific, European settlement was coming to New Zealand and Australia, displacing Maoris and Aborigines.

The rise of new hopes

In 1783 a strange shape rose into the sky over Paris. It was the world's first hot-air balloon, built by the Montgolfier brothers. As it ascended with three passengers – a sheep, a cock and a duck – King Louis XVI and Queen Marie-Antoinette of France were among the astonished spectators (see also page 50).

Scientists were pushing back the frontiers of knowledge (see right). The revolution in science seemed to offer reasoned answers to many questions. It also helped bring about the 'age of machines' – the Industrial Revolution – that promised both power and profit.

In Britain, in 1775, James Watt and Matthew Boulton set up a company to make steam engines. Earlier, the steam engine had been used to pump water from mines. Watt redesigned it to make it work better, so that machinery in factories and mills could be driven much faster to speed up industrial production (see below).

▶ THE POWER OF STEAM

The Scottish engineer James Watt did not invent the steam engine. But the improvements that he made to its design transformed technology and, in turn, the Western economy. The first steam engines were inefficient and their up-and-down motion was useful only for pumping water. In 1774 Watt patented a more powerful engine with a separate condenser, and seven years later he adapted it for circular motion. By the turn of the century, Watt engines were driving factory machines, land vehicles and the first steamships, which used paddle-wheels for their propulsion.

▲ THE FIRST CHEMIST

Lavoisier, the father of modern chemistry

Antoine Lavoisier (1743–1794) of France was the first chemist to carry out experiments showing what happened when a substance burns. He discovered that combustion (burning) needs oxygen, the gas discovered by Priestley (see page 46). Lavoisier also studied the way in which animals breathe, and he developed the system for naming chemical substances, based on their composition, that is used today. A member of the government, he was arrested during the French Revolution and sent to the guillotine.

James Watt with a steam engine

1770–1780	1780–1789
1770s Lavoisier in France, Priestley and Rutherford in Britain, and Schule in Germany discover the gases that exist in air. **1771** In Britain, Richard Arkwright starts first mechanized factory. **1775** Start of American War of Independence. **1775** Watt and Boulton start their company to make steam engines. **1776** American colonies declare independence.	**1783** First balloon flight by people, in Paris. Britain recognizes independence of United States of America. **1785** First balloon flight across English Channel by Blanchard. **1788** First convicts transported from Britain to Australia. **1789** Start of French Revolution. **1789** George Washington chosen as first President of the United States.

51

First fleet to Australia

Captain Cook, who had sailed to Australia (see page 44), made two further voyages of exploration, between 1772 and 1779. He became the first explorer to cross the Antarctic Circle and to witness the forbidding pack ice around Antarctica. Cook also discovered Hawaii and explored the northern Pacific, while in search of the North-West Passage sea route that was believed to lie between Asia and Europe. But there was no way open through the northern ice. Returning to Hawaii, Cook was killed there after quarrelling with the islanders.

The voyages of explorers such as Cook and the Frenchman Louis de Bougainville, who sailed round the world and wrote a book about it, had solved many mysteries. There was no second Asia, with a rich history of civilization, only near-empty Australia and the islands of the Pacific. Australia was so remote that the British government decided it would make an ideal penal colony. Some of the prisoners who went there had been found guilty of only small crimes, but all of them were sentenced to be transported for life (see page 53).

In the 18th century, Britain's population doubled to 10 million. Some economists who believed that overpopulation in Europe was a problem saw emigration to places such as Australia and New Zealand (see page 53) as a possible solution. In 1776 a Scottish economist named Adam Smith wrote that, to cope with more people, the wealth of nations needed to be increased by self-interest. He believed that business should operate freely without government interference.

EUROPE	ASIA	AFRICA, PACIFIC	AMERICA
1770 Smallpox epidemic hits Europe. **1771** Russia occupies Crimea; this is accepted by Turkey in 1784. **1773** Cossack leader Pugachev leads unsuccessful revolt against Catherine the Great. **1774** Louis XVI becomes King of France (to 1792). **1778** War of Bavarian Succession between Austria and Prussia. **1778** France sides with Americans against Britain. **1779** Britain and Spain at war. **1780** Gordon riots (anti-Catholic) in London. **1781** Joseph II introduces reforms (religious toleration, end of serfdom) in Austrian Empire. **1783** Montgolfiers demonstrate hot-air ballooning in France. **1787** Russia and Turkey at war. **1789** French Revolution begins with the calling of the Estates General and the fall of the Bastille.	**1771** First dissection of human body in Japan by doctors, using a Dutch textbook as a guide. **1771** Shah Alam is Mogul emperor, kept in power by the Marathas. **1774** British government appoints Warren Hastings as first Governor-General of India. **1775** War between British and Marathas, lasting until 1782. **1777** First Christian missions to Korea. **1783** Pitt's India Act gives the British government control of the East India Company in India. **1787** Famine in Japan leads to food riots.	**1771** Cook returns to England after his first voyage of exploration. **1775** British explorer James Bruce comes back from a journey into Ethiopia, exploring the Blue Nile. **1775** Cook completes his second voyage, having sailed round Antarctica and discovered the South Sandwich Islands. **1776** Cook sets out on his third and last voyage to the Pacific, seeking the North-West Passage. **1778** Dutch settlers move west of the Fish River into African-held lands. This leads to fighting. **1779** Cook is killed by islanders in Hawaii. **1786** Turkish troops invade Egypt to quell the independence of the Mameluke rulers there. **1787** Sierra Leone founded as colony for freed American slaves. **1788** First fleet carrying convict-settlers from Britain arrives in Australia.	**1770** Boston Massacre rouses colonists against British. **1773** Boston Tea Party. **1775** Fighting begins at Lexington and Concord. Battle of Bunker Hill. **1776** American leaders sign Declaration of Independence. **1776** South America: Spain welds Argentina, Bolivia, Paraguay and Uruguay into the new Vice-Royalty of Rio de la Plata. **1777** Battle of Saratoga: American victory over British. **1780–83** Peruvian Indians led by Inca Tupac Amaru revolt against Spain. **1781** British army surrenders to the Americans at Yorktown, Virginia. **1783** Peace of Paris ends American Revolution. **1787** The Constitution of the United States is adopted, uniting the colonies as a federal republic. **1789** George Washington is the United States' first president.

Early Australian settlers

⬤ SETTLEMENT OF AUSTRALIA

In January 1788 a fleet of British convict ships dropped anchor in Botany Bay, New South Wales. According to Captain Cook's earlier survey of the coastline, Australia was green and fertile, but Cook did not see the vast deserts farther inland. The first convict-colonists faced a hard time in this strange land, with its unfamiliar climate and its exotic animals. But somehow they coped. They built farms and houses, and from this small beginning a new nation grew.

▶ THE MAORIS OF NEW ZEALAND

A Maori village

The first people to settle New Zealand were the Maoris, who came by canoe, probably from Polynesia. When the Europeans explored the coasts of New Zealand, in the 1600s and 1700s, the Maoris had lived there for some 800 years. They farmed and they fished, and were also expert hunters. The Maoris were often at war with each other and lived in fortified villages. They built large, brightly coloured meeting houses and decorated them with carvings.

SOCIETY, SCIENCE

1771 John Howard calls for reform of British prisons.
1774 German writer Goethe's 'romantic' novel *The Sorrows of Young Werther*.
1776 Tom Paine's pamphlet *Common Sense*.
1776 The French Marquis d'Abbans tests a steam-driven boat.
1776 Economist Adam Smith's book *The Wealth of Nations*.
1777 Paris has its first daily newspaper.
1779 Thomas Chippendale, English furniture-maker, dies.
1779 First iron bridge, at Coalbrookdale, England.
1780 Galvani of Italy shows that frogs' bodies have electrical activity.
1782 William Herschel discovers planet Uranus.
1783 French chemist Lavoisier combines hydrogen and oxygen to make water.
1783 Montgolfier balloon carries two aeronauts.
1787 Mozart's opera *Don Giovanni* first performed.
1788 London *Times* published.

▶ TOM PAINE – REVOLUTIONARY

A cartoon of 'Mad' Tom Paine

In the West the old order was crumbling. Revolutionaries in Europe and America called for equality, liberty and justice for all. Among these was the Englishman Tom Paine. Poor and uneducated, Paine was befriended by Ben Franklin (see page 43) and went to America. There he wrote a stirring pamphlet, *Common Sense*, urging Americans to break with Britain. Paine saw his dream of American independence come true, then went to France. He became a French citizen and wrote *The Rights of Man*, a fierce defence of the French Revolution. He returned to America, where, disillusioned, he died in poverty in 1809.

Revolutions of common sense

In North America there was plenty of enterprise, but some of the wealth created went to Britain. Many people in the 13 colonies did not want to be bound by laws made in Britain by a Parliament in which they were not represented. They especially disliked paying taxes to Britain.

In Europe demands for democracy fell on deaf ears. European empires were autocracies, such as Russia, whose ruler Catherine the Great (see right) harshly put down uprisings by oppressed peasants who challenged her power.

Britain was not strong enough to rule a worldwide empire, as it later did, but still it would not share government with the colonists. The British acted clumsily. Giving the Americans more say in their own affairs would probably have ended the grumbling. Instead, the unrest grew worse and America moved towards revolution.

The Empress Catherine

ⓐ CATHERINE THE GREAT

Catherine the Great ruled Russia for 34 years, until her death in 1796. She was not Russian but German, and became tsarina (empress) after her mad husband, Tsar Peter, was murdered by army officers. The army made Catherine ruler of Russia, and she rewarded her soldiers by doing all she could to enlarge Russia's territory through wars. Catherine expressed concern about the plight of Russia's downtrodden serfs, but did little to help them because she knew this would anger the nobles. So instead she encouraged learning and Western European culture. She wrote a history of her adopted country, collected paintings and was a tireless writer of letters to scholars and intellectuals all over Europe.

The Boston Massacre

◀ UNREST IN AMERICA

America moved almost reluctantly towards revolution. The colonies' leaders, like George Washington and Thomas Jefferson, were gentlemen-farmers, not rabble-rousers. Yet Americans had grievances. They wanted more land, more trade with foreign countries and fewer taxes. Instead of listening, the British government sent ships and troops to keep order. In 1770 British soldiers in Boston opened fire on a crowd, killing five people. The 'Boston Massacre', as it became known, provided the spark to ignite the powder keg of rebellion. When Britain offered Americans cargoes of cheap tea in 1773, American patriots, disguised as Indians, threw the tea into Boston harbour. This was the so-called 'Boston Tea Party'. By 1775 Britain and America were at war.

At first, few Americans wanted a clean break with Britain, but radicals like the writer Tom Paine (see page 53) convinced them that only independence would secure the rights and freedoms they sought. In July 1776 the American Congress adopted the Declaration of Independence. Its message, that 'all men are created equal', echoed around the world.

A new mood in France

The American revolution (see pages 56–57) provided a thrilling but dangerous example for people in Europe to follow.

France had strongly supported the American rebels. But wars are expensive, and France was almost bankrupt. King Louis XVI's advisers told him to raise money from new taxes. As France had no parliament, Louis decided to obtain agreement for new taxes by calling together the Estates General, an assembly that had not met since 1614.

The Estates General met again in 1789. Its members represented three groups, called 'estates', in French society. The clergy and nobles made up the First and Second Estates, which together numbered about half a million people. The Third Estate was more than 20 million strong. It included middle-class merchants and lawyers as well as poor peasants who were uneducated and who often went hungry. The middle classes, encouraged by the writings of Rousseau and Voltaire (see pages 46, 47) wanted reforms. The poor wanted bread and lower taxes.

In April 1789 George Washington became President of the new republic of the United States of America. In June 1789 the representatives of France's Third Estate swore not to disband until France had a new system of government. Three weeks later a mob stormed the hated Bastille prison in Paris. America's war for freedom had inspired revolution in the heart of Europe.

⏵ THE FRENCH REVOLUTION

At the meeting of France's Three Estates in 1789 the king asked the representatives to write down their grievances. The list was endless. The Third Estate, led by a lawyer, Mirabeau, called for a new system of government giving more power to the Third Estate. Paris bubbled with expectation and there was great excitement on the streets. People seized weapons and, on 14 July, a mob attacked the Bastille. The fall of the city's ancient fortress-prison marked the beginning of the end for the king and for the old France.

The storming of the Bastille

AMERICAN INDEPENDENCE

The war between Britain and its American colonies resulted from the Americans' growing anger at the way they were being governed. Protests such as the Boston Tea Party (see page 54) were met by harsh punishments – the closure of Boston port and the forced billeting (lodging) of British soldiers in American homes. In 1774 delegates from the 13 American colonies met and decided to end trade with Britain.

In 1775 fighting began at Lexington and Concord in Massachusetts. Colonial leaders met and organized an army. At its head was George Washington, who had learned soldiering in the French and Indian War (see page 42). The colonial leaders drafted a document declaring the United States of America to be independent. A few Americans remained loyal to Britain.

Victory and independence

The British conducted the war badly, even though they had an army of about 50,000 regular soldiers and a strong navy with which to blockade American ports. The Americans, however, were on their home ground and inspired by patriotism, whereas many on the British side were hired German troops. The Americans won an important victory at Saratoga in 1777. After this, France entered the war, and British forces had to be diverted to fight off the French.

The last battle, at Yorktown in 1781, ended in a British surrender. Peace talks began, and the war was officially concluded by the Treaty of Paris in 1783. The American Revolution had succeeded. The newly formed republic of the United States of America adopted its Constitution in 1787.

Saratoga
Charleston
Boston
Philadelphia
Providence
Yorktown
Norfolk

British Proclamation Line 1763

● US victory   ● British victory

△ In 1763 a British Proclamation banned colonists from settling west of the Appalachians. In the Revolutionary War, Britain hoped to defeat the Americans by a naval blockade and by seizing northern cities. Britain expected less resistance in the south, but there the Americans won the war.

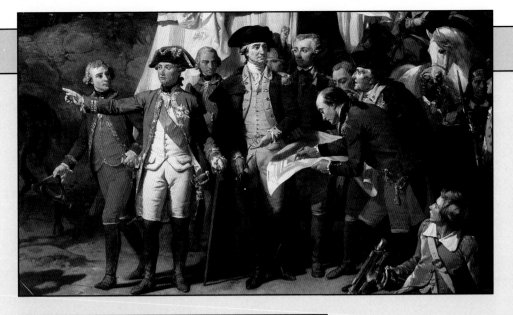

◁ The siege of Yorktown, 1781. Rochambeau and Washington, leading the combined French and American forces, ordered the attack on the trapped British army of Cornwallis. The British surrendered on 19 October 1781. Scattered fighting went on for two more years, but the war was really over.

THE REVOLUTIONARY WAR

1775 American 'minutemen' militia clash with British soldiers at Lexington and Concord; war begins. Battle of Bunker Hill is a costly British victory.
1776–77 British capture New York, and then Philadelphia, but lose badly at Saratoga.
1777 Washington leads American army to winter quarters at Valley Forge: many die or desert.
1778–79 France and Spain enter war on America's side.
1779 John Paul Jones captures British ship *Serapis*.
1780 American general Benedict Arnold goes over to British side.
1781 French defeat British fleet at Chesapeake Bay. British commander Cornwallis surrenders his army (about 8,000 men) at Yorktown, Virginia.
1783 Peace treaty is signed in Paris.

△ Part of the American Constitution, drawn up in 1787 after the war. It set down the new united nation's fundamental laws.

(Left) George Washington encourages his troops at Valley Forge, 1777. Washington turned part-time volunteers, including freed slaves, into a disciplined army. In winter camp at Valley Forge, Pennsylvania, one in four soldiers died of cold and disease.

CHANGES

The Age of Discovery was a period of great changes. Peoples from different continents came into contact with each other. Explorers sailed the oceans. The Renaissance and the Reformation changed the way people thought about themselves and their world.

The Renaissance

The Renaissance brought about the end of the Middle Ages and the start of modern times. It reached its peak in Europe in about 1500. It was a time of discovery in the arts and sciences when people were eager to find out more about the world around them. The desire to know more and to increase wealth spurred people to undertake long voyages across unknown oceans. The centre of the Renaissance was Italy, where some of the greatest-ever painters, sculptors and architects lived. Instead of accepting ancient beliefs as they had done before, people began to observe and experiment for themselves. Scientists showed the Earth was not the centre of the Universe. They studied the stars and examined animals and plants, to find out how things worked.

Discovery

When Columbus 'discovered' the New World of America in 1492, the people already living there had their own civilizations and empires. But they did not have horses or guns, and this made it easy for invaders to conquer them. The Europeans took their lands and stole their gold. Slaves from Africa were shipped to the New World. But so too were the Pilgrim Fathers, who came to find freedom from the persecutions of the Old World. Colonies were founded, the seeds of new nations – Canada, the United States, Brazil. Eager for trade and wealth, Europeans also settled in Africa, India and Indonesia. They also tried to gain footholds in Japan and China, and began to colonize Australia and New Zealand.

Reformation

Until the 1500s the Christian Church in western Europe was a single organization, run from Rome. The Reformation was a movement for reform, a protest against corruption that had become widespread. Its leaders were Luther, Calvin and Zwingli. The breakaway Protestant Churches made the Bible available in languages other than Latin, so that ordinary people could understand it. But the Reformation also led to terrible wars of religion in Europe.

EUROPE

1500 Renaissance at its height in Italy.
1517 Start of Protestant Reformation in Europe.
1519–22 First round-the-world voyage, by Magellan's crew.
1524 Peasants' War in Germany.
1534 Henry VIII makes himself head of the Church in England.
1543 Polish astronomer Copernicus shows that the Earth orbits the Sun.
1545–63 Council of Trent; the Counter-Reformation.
1556 Philip II becomes King of Spain and Netherlands.
1558–1603 Elizabeth I Queen of England.
1564 Births of Shakespeare, Galileo.
1568 Dutch revolt against Spanish rule.
1571 Battle of Lepanto.
1572 Massacre of Protestants in France.
1577 Drake's round-the-world voyage (to 1580).
1577 Rubens, Flemish painter, born.
1581 Foundation of Dutch Republic, under William the Silent.
1582 Pope Gregory XIII's reformed calendar.
1585 Religious wars in France.
1588 England defeats Spain's Armada.
1590 Invention of microscope by Janssen (Netherlands).

William Shakespeare
1564–1616

1590–1613 Shakespeare writing his plays.
1598 Edict of Nantes brings religious peace to France.
1605 Cervantes, Spanish writer, publishes first part of *Don Quixote*.
1607 First opera, by Italian composer Monteverdi.
1609 Galileo uses telescope to study the Moon and planets.
1618 Start of Thirty Years' War in Germany.
1642 Start of English Civil War.
1643 Louis XIV King of France.
1648 Fronde uprising in France.

ASIA AND RUSSIA

1500 Ismail I founds Safavid dynasty in Persia.
1520 Suleiman the Magnificent becomes Ottoman sultan.
1526 Foundation of Mogul Empire in India by Babur.
1526 Ottoman Turks defeat Louis II of Bohemia and Hungary at battle of Mohacs.
1529 Suleiman the Magnificent besieges Vienna, but is driven back.
1534 Turks capture Baghdad and Mesopotamia.
1540s Portuguese are first Europeans to land in Japan.

Ivan the Terrible
1530–1585

1547 Ivan the Terrible crowned Tsar of Russia.
1549 First Christian mission to Japan.
1565 Akbar extends Mogul rule into southern India.
1575 Akbar conquers Bengal.
1581 Russian settlement of Siberia begins.
1582 Hideyoshi becomes ruler of Japan.
1584 Siam (modern Thailand) becomes independent under Phra Narai.
1587 Shah Abbas I becomes ruler of Persia.
1600 English East India Company founded.
1627 Shah Jahan ruler of Mogul India.
1629 Death of Shah Abbas ends the greatest period of Safavid Persia's prosperity.
1638 Russian expansion eastward brings them to the Pacific.
1641 Japan cuts itself off from foreign contact; expels Christian missionaries.
1649 Serfdom enforced by law in Russia.

AMERICA

1501 Portuguese begin exploration of Brazil.
1502 Columbus makes fourth and last voyage to America.
1503 Spanish conquer Puerto Rico.
1507 The name America is first used on a map of the world.
1509 First Spanish settlement of American mainland.
1513 Balboa sights Pacific Ocean.
1515 Spanish complete conquest of Cuba.
1520 Spanish missionaries begin converting American Indians to Christianity, mostly by force.
1521 Cortes conquers the Aztecs of Mexico.
1525 Civil war among Incas in Peru.
1532 Portuguese begin settlement of Brazil.
1532 Pizarro leads Spanish invasion of Inca empire.
1535 Spaniards complete conquest of Incas.
1535 Cartier explores the St Lawrence River in Canada.
1540s Spanish move into American Southwest.
1564 Silver shipments from America to Spain begin.
1579 Drake is first European to see west coast of Canada.
1583 Gilbert founds English colony in Newfoundland.
1605 French settle Nova Scotia.
1607 English found a colony at Jamestown in Virginia.
1620 Pilgrim Fathers land in Plymouth, Massachusetts.
1642 French found settlement at Montreal in Canada.

Champlain's House, Quebec

CHINA AND AUSTRALASIA

1500s An age of philosophical discussion in China.
1557 Portuguese set up trading base at Macao, China.
1582 Matteo Ricci, Jesuit priest, arrives in China.
1592 China aids Korea against Japanese attack.
1606 Willem Jansz, a Dutch navigator, and De Torres of Spain are the first Europeans to sight Australia.
1616 Willem Schouten of Holland sails round Cape Horn into the Pacific.

Ming statue 16th century

1616 Manchu leader Nurbuchi proclaims a new dynasty.
1620s Manchus raid China, across the Great Wall.
1624 Chinese emperor Hsi-tung, a weak ruler.
1642 Abel Tasman of Holland sees Van Diemen's Land (Tasmania) and New Zealand.
1644 Collapse of Ming dynasty in China; Manchus take over.

Abel Tasman in Tonga 1640s

AFRICA

1500 First African slaves taken to America to work in Spanish-run plantations and mines in West Indies and South America. During the 1500s the slave trade to the New World grows steadily.

African slaves

1505 Portuguese establish trading posts in East Africa. They win control of the East African city-states during the 1500s.

Benin bronze of Portuguese trader

1517 Ottoman Turks invade and capture Egypt. North Africa is a Muslim-ruled region and Muslim power stretches south across the Sahara Desert.
1546 Destruction of Mali Empire by its rival Songhai.
1562 English become active in slave trade, shipping slaves from Sierra Leone to Hispaniola.
1571 Bornu Empire in West Africa under Sultan Idris.
1578 Moroccans defeat Portuguese.
1591 Moroccans with European mercenaries defeat Songhai. End of Songhai power.
1600s Dutch take over many of Portugal's trading posts on west coast of Africa. English traders also set up bases.

REVOLUTIONS

Arts
After the Renaissance, Western art moved through several styles. In the 1600s the highly decorated Baroque and Rococo styles affected architecture, painting and music. Then artists turned to Neoclassicism, a return to the simpler forms of ancient Greece and Rome. In the East art and architecture flourished in the Muslim empires and in China and Japan. Chinese art, especially pottery, became fashionable in Europe. The 1500s were a great age of drama, with Shakespeare and other European dramatists. Most Western literature was in the form of poetry until the appearance, in the 1600s, of a popular story-telling form in prose: the novel. Some novels were in the form of correspondence; others recounted a series of adventures involving a hero or heroine. In music, the opera, ballet and symphony all developed at this time. By the end of the 1700s the Romantic movement was beginning .

Science and industry
Scientific progress was rapid, particularly in physics and mathematics. There were also advances in biology, medicine and chemistry. Engineers designed machinery to do work previously done by people, such as weaving and spinning. Iron was made in greater quantities by new processes, and by the end of the 1700s there were steam engines and balloons that could carry people. The Industrial Revolution changed people's lives. Instead of working at home, many people were forced to find jobs in towns, in the new factories.

Freedom and equality
The new ideas during the Age of Discovery made people restless. Most had no say in how they were governed. Kings and nobles still ruled in most countries. But now reformers demanded democracy – government by the people. They believed in the 'rights of man' and called for the end of evils such as slavery. This demand for change helped bring about the revolutions in America and France, whose impact was felt all over the world.

EUROPE

1650s–1660s Plague kills many people in Europe.
1653 Oliver Cromwell Lord Protector of England.
1661 Louis XIV absolute monarch of France.
1670s Anton van Leeuwenhoek uses microscope to study microbes.
1683 John Sobieski saves Vienna from Turks.
1687 Newton publishes laws of motion.
1700–21 Great Northern War between Sweden and Russia, Denmark and Poland.
1701–13 War of Spanish Succession.
1709 Abraham Darby pioneers coke-smelting of iron.
1733 John Kay invents the flying shuttle.
1733 War of Polish Succession: France and Spain against Russia and Austria.
1740–8 War of Austrian Succession.

J.S. Bach 1685-1750

1750 J.S. Bach, German composer, dies.
1756 Prussia invades Saxony, starts Seven Years' War.
1756 Austrian composer Mozart born.
1763 Treaty of Paris ends Seven Years' War.
1764 Hargreaves's spinning jenny.
1765 Joseph II emperor of Austria.
1766 Cavendish discovers hydrogen gas.
1770 Births of Wordsworth, English Romantic writer and Beethoven, German composer.
1772 Poland split between Russia, Prussia and Austria.
1781 Joseph II abolishes serfdom in Austrian Empire.
1782 Watt's improved steam engine.
1782 Planet Uranus discovered.
1789 Start of French Revolution.

ASIA AND RUSSIA

1650 Economic growth in Japan; plays and novels popular.
1653 In India, the Taj Mahal is finished.
1657 Shah Jahan, Mogul emperor, succeeded by Aurangzeb.
1669 Hindus face persecution in Mogul India.
1674 Sivaji, Hindu leader, defeats Moguls.
1680s Russian expansion begins under Peter the Great.
1690 Founding of Calcutta in India by English traders.
1707 Death of Aurangzeb, Mogul emperor of India.
1709 Afghans revolt against Persian rule.
1736 In Persia, Nadir Shah overthrows Safavid dynasty.
1739 Nadir Shah captures Delhi in India.

Nadir Shah,
ruler of Persia from 1736

1740s Beginning of British–French rivalry in India.
1747 Kingdom of Afghanistan founded.
1755 Burmese found new capital at Rangoon.
1756 British and French at war in India.
1757 Battle of Plassey in India.
1761 Battle of Panipat: Afghans defeat Mogul emperor.
1762 Catherine the Great becomes Russian ruler.
1774 Warren Hastings first governor-general of India.
1775–82 War between British and Marathas in India.
1777 First Christian missions to Korea.
1783 India Act gives British government control of the East India Company in India.

AMERICA

1650s French begin colonization of Canada.
1664 English take New Amsterdam from Dutch.
1670 English found the Hudson's Bay Company.
1702–13 Queen Anne's War, fought by Europeans in North America, with Indian allies.
1730s Europeans explore the Great Plains and see the Rocky Mountains.
1742 Peruvian Indians revolt against Spanish rule.
1740s–1760s Britain and France at war for North America.
1759 British take Quebec.
1763 Chief Pontiac leads Indian uprising in Great Lakes region.
1763 Rio de Janeiro becomes capital of Brazil.
1763 Britain gains French Canada.
1770 Boston Massacre.
1773 Boston Tea Party.

Boston Tea Party

1775 War of Independence starts in American colonies.
1776 American Declaration of Independence.
1780–3 Peruvian Indians led by Inca Tupac Amaru revolt against Spain.
1781 British surrender to Americans at Yorktown. Americans loyal to Britain move north to Canada.
1783 Peace of Paris ends American Revolution.
1787 The Constitution of the United States is adopted uniting the colonies as a federal republic.
1789 George Washington is the United States' first President.

CHINA AND AUSTRALASIA

1661 Second Manchu emperor Kang-hsi is the most enlightened ruler of his age. Jesuit missionaries attend his court.
1662 Koxinga (Cheng Ch'eng-kung) seizes Taiwan for Ming rebels.
1680s Waterway improvements in China.
1685 Manchus defeat Koxinga.
1697 Chinese occupy Outer Mongolia.

Manchu Summer Palace 1644

1717 First accurate atlas of Chinese empire.
1720 Chinese send troops to garrison Tibet.
1722 Death of Chinese emperor Kang-hsi.
1722 Jacob Roggeveen of Holland discovers Easter Island.
1725 Vitus Bering, a Dane, explores the eastern Pacific for Russia.
1736 Fourth Manchu emperor Chien-lung begins 60-year reign.
1765 Chinese invade Burma.
1766 Louis de Bougainville of France sets sail on round-the-world voyage.
1766 Samuel Wallis (Britain) discovers the Society Islands (Tahiti).
1768 James Cook of Britain begins his first voyage to the Pacific.
1770 Cook lands in New South Wales, Australia.
1775 Cook completes his second voyage.
1779 Cook is killed by islanders in Hawaii.
1788 First British settlement of Australia.

AFRICA

1652 First European settlement in South Africa, by Dutch at Cape Town.
1650s In West Africa's Gold Coast European countries compete for gold and slave trade.
1659 French found trading station on coast of Senegal.
1662 Portuguese destroy Kongo kingdom.
1670 Mandingos overthrown in Niger region.
1680s–1690s Portuguese lose control of East African strongholds to local African rulers and Arabs.
1700 Asante power grows in West Africa.
1731 Oyo (Yoruba) Empire in West Africa defeats Dahomey.

Yoruba carving 17-18th century

1760s West Africa increasingly Islamic. North Africa and much of East Africa also Muslim-ruled.
1775 Scot James Bruce explores Ethiopia and the Blue Nile river. Most of Africa's interior still a mystery to Westerners, although Arabs know large areas of it.
1778 In the Cape colony Dutch settlers clash with neighbouring Africans.
1786 Turkey invades Egypt to end independence of the Mameluke rulers there.
1787 Sierra Leone settlement for freed American slaves.

GLOSSARY

absolute ruler One who is all-powerful.

alliance An agreement between two or more countries to help one another, often in war.

astronomer A scientist who studies the stars and planets.

bankruptcy Being without money to pay debts.

cannon Heavy guns used by armies and warships.

cardinal A high-ranking member of the Roman Catholic Church.

caravan A group of merchants travelling together for safety.

civil war A war between different groups within a country.

colony A settlement of people establishing their way of life in another country.

convict A person sent to prison or banished for a crime.

diplomacy The means by which countries deal with one another, by bargaining.

dynasty Ruling family, one generation succeeding another.

empire A large territory ruled by an emperor or king, and reaching far beyond the ruler's homeland.

galleon A sailing ship with three masts and **cannon**.

halberd A weapon like a long spear with an axe head.

heresy An idea or belief that is against accepted teachings.

Hinduism An ancient religion of India.

Holy Roman Empire An area covering Germany, the Netherlands, Austria, Bohemia and northern Italy which grew out of Charlemgne's empire (800–840). The last Holy Roman Emperor gave up the title in 1806.

Huguenots French Protestants.

Inquisition The organization in the Roman Catholic Church for seeking out **heresy**.

Islam The religion founded by the Prophet Muhammad (died in 632).

Jacobites Supporters of the Stuart cause in Britain after 1689.

Jesuits An order of **missionary** priests.

missionaries People seeking to convert others to their religious beliefs.

Mongols A warlike people originally from central Asia.

monks and nuns Members of religious orders, living and worshipping in monasteries.

musket An early handgun, looking like a long rifle.

Muslim A follower of the religion of **Islam**.

New World The name given to the Americas by Europeans.

noble An aristocrat, a landowner with a title, such as duke.

Old World Europe, Asia and Africa.

Ottoman Empire The empire based on Turkey with its capital at Istanbul.

peasant A poor person working as a farm labourer, sometimes owning small plots of land.

pike A long spear used by foot soldiers.

pirates Sea bandits roving the Caribbean and Mediterranean seas and the Indian Ocean.

plantation Farm in the New World for growing sugar, tobacco, coffee, or cotton.

radical A person with advanced ideas, a believer in progress.

reform Changes, especially to government.

Reformation The protest movement that divided the Christian Church in the 1500s.

republic A form of government without a king or queen.

revolt An attempt by people to overthrow their rulers.

settlement A place where people live and build homes.

Shah The title used by Persian and other Muslim rulers.

shogun A military ruler in Japan.

slaves People forced to work for someone against their will.

treaty An agreement between countries or rulers.

Tsar A ruler of the Russian Empire (before 1917).

INDEX

Acknowledgements
Designer: Ben White
Project Editor: Lionel Bender
Text Editor: Mike March
Picture Researcher: Jennie Karrach
Media Conversion and Typesetting:
    Peter MacDonald and Una Macnamara
Managing Editor: David Riley
All maps by Hayward Art Group.

Picture credits
Title page, Page 3: Lionel Bender. Page 11: Sonia
Halliday Photographs. Page 13: The National Gallery,
London. Page 16: Hatfield House. Page 20: Michael
Holford. Page 26: National Maritime Museum,
London. Pages 27,29: Michael Holford. Page 35: Ann
Ronan Picture Library. Page 41: ZEFA. Pages 44,49:
e.t. archive. Page 50: Mary Evans Picture Library.
Page 53: The Mansell Collection. Pages 55, 57: The
Bridgeman Art Library.
Cover: Michael Holford, The Mansell Collection.